HEALING A GRANDPARENT'S
GRIEVING HEART

Also by Alan Wolfelt:

Healing a Parent's Grieving Heart:
100 Practical Ideas After Your Child Dies

Understanding Your Grief:
Ten Essential Touchstones for Finding
Hope and Healing Your Heart

Healing A Friend's Grieving Heart:
100 Practical Ideas for Helping Someone You Love Through Loss

Healing Your Grieving Heart:
100 Practical Ideas

Loving From the Outside In,
Mourning From the Inside Out

The Journey Through Grief:
Reflections on Healing

The Mourner's Book of Hope:
30 Days of Inspiration

*Companion Press is dedicated to the education
and support of both the bereaved and bereavement
caregivers. We believe that those who companion
the bereaved by walking with them as they journey
in grief have a wondrous opportunity: to help others
embrace and grow through grief—and to lead
fuller, more deeply-lived lives themselves
because of this important ministry.*

Companion
P R E S S

For a complete catalog and ordering information, write or call:

Companion Press
The Center for Loss and Life Transition
3735 Broken Bow Road
Fort Collins, CO 80526
(970) 226-6050
www.centerforloss.com

HEALING A GRANDPARENT'S GRIEVING HEART

•

100 PRACTICAL IDEAS AFTER YOUR GRANDCHILD DIES

•

ALAN D. WOLFELT, PH.D.

Companion
PRESS

Fort Collins, Colorado

An imprint of the Center for Loss and Life Transition

Companion Press is an imprint of the
Center for Loss and Life Transition,
3735 Broken Bow Road
Fort Collins, Colorado 80526
www.centerforloss.com

21 20 19 18 17 16 15 14   5 4 3 2 1

ISBN: 978-1-61722-197-2

In Gratitude

*To the grandparents who have invited me
to walk with them through the wilderness of their grief.
What you have taught me is what I feel honored to pass on
to others. Thank you for entrusting me with the love stories
surrounding your children and grandchildren.*

CONTENTS

INTRODUCTION

*"It's such a grand thing to be a parent of a parent.
That's why we call them grandparents."*

— Author unknown

Your precious grandchild has died. In my decades as a grief counselor and educator, I have had the privilege to companion many, many grieving parents and grandparents. They have taught me that when a child or grandchild dies, it's as if a deep hole implodes inside of you. The hole seems to penetrate you and leaves you gasping for air.

I hope the words I express from my heart to yours throughout the following pages help you to mourn well so that you can go on to live and love well again. I realize that no book can take your overwhelming loss away. It rages in the recesses of your soul. Your profound loss will endure, and nothing I can say or do will alter that truth.

Yet I truly believe that acknowledging your heart is broken is the beginning of your healing. As you experience the pain of your loss—gently opening, acknowledging, and allowing—the suffering it has wrought diminishes but never completely vanishes. In fact, the resistance to the pain can potentially be more painful than the pain itself. Running from the pain of loss closes down our hearts and spirits. As difficult as it is, we must relinquish ourselves to the pain of grief. As Helen Keller said, "The only way to the other side is through."

Grandparents grieve twice

While I am not yet a grandparent, I hope to be one someday. My three beautiful children are, at the time of this writing, in their late teens and early twenties, and though it's sometimes hard for me to believe, I will turn sixty this year. So though I speak to you not as someone who has lived your experience, I am a parent and I am eligible for AARP credentials. I have also spent the last

30-plus years following my life's calling to educate others about the natural and necessary process we call grief.

What I know about the unique grief of grandparents is this: You grieve doubly. You grieve for the loss of your grandchild, and you grieve for your child whose child has died.

You've probably heard the saying that to be a parent is to forever have your heart walking around outside your body. We love our children more than anything, and from the moment they are born, it is our instinct—and our privilege—to protect and teach them.

Yet you could not protect your child from the death of her child. So now she aches, and you ache for her. You would like to take her pain away, but you cannot.

Of course, if you had a relationship with the grandchild who died (and I'm guessing that if you are reading this book, you did!), you also ache. Someone very special to you has died, and you grieve.

Grandparents grieve twice. The word "grandparent" comes from the French word *grand*, meaning "great" or "big." This word and the customs of many cultures tell us that grandparents are the "great" parents—that is, they are the matriarchs and patriarchs of the family. They are wise, and in some ways, we see them as responsible for their entire families. So even as you are grieving twice, you may well feel that you should be "strong" and "in control." As you will learn in this little book, your healing depends not on feigned "strength" but instead on expressing your authentic thoughts and feelings.

Forgotten mourners

When a child or young person dies, friends and family members usually focus their sympathy and support on the parents of the child who died. Next to be comforted are the siblings of the child who died. Grieving grandparents, on the other hand, are often neglected or forgotten.

What makes this predicament especially hard for grieving grandparents is that they typically *want* their grieving child and grieving grandchildren to be supported as much as possible. They don't want to shine the grief spotlight on themselves, because their love for their child and grandchildren demands selflessness.

Yet all the while, grieving grandparents are often experiencing profound suffering, silently and alone. If you are a forgotten mourner in the aftermath of your grandchild's death, I am glad you are reading this book. Find ways to mourn and be supported outside your immediate family. You need and deserve your own support, and besides, the better you yourself are supported, the more able you will be to help your grieving child and grandchildren.

An out-of-order death

Further complicating grandparents' grief is the horrible reality that a young person died before they did. Children aren't supposed to die before their parents, and they certainly are not supposed to die before their grandparents. This death is unnatural, untimely, and out of order, which results in some grandparents experiencing feelings of guilt as part of their grief journeys.

Many grieving grandparents have told me that they would gladly have swapped places with the child who died if they could have. Do you feel this way? If you feel guilty and regretful since the death, you may understand that while these feelings are not logical (of course you have nothing to "legitimately" feel guilty about!), they are still very real. Finding ways to share these natural and understandable feelings with others will help them soften and dissipate.

If you are grieving a miscarriage or stillbirth

The grieving grandparents I have been honored to companion have taught me that few events in life bring about such warm and wonderful feelings of anticipation as the announcement of a pregnancy. As soon as you and your family learn a baby is on the way, you naturally begin to have hopes and dreams for the future. These hopes and dreams take on a life of their own and begin to grow inside you, even as the baby is growing inside his mother. Yet when you come to grief, there is no longer a living baby to go with your hopes and dreams.

If you are grieving a miscarriage or stillbirth, you will find that while many of the ideas in this book apply to you, they may need to be modified. You may not have photos to display, for example, or memories of time spent together. Instead, perhaps you have ultrasound pictures and imagined moments together, both of which you can use and express in healing ways. I would also encourage you and your grieving child to read my book *Healing Your Grieving Heart After Stillbirth*.

How to use this book

Whether your grandchild was very young when she died or an independent adult (perhaps with a family of her own); whether the death was the result of an illness, an accident, a homicide, or suicide; whether the death was sudden or lingering; the messages I am honored to bring you in this book are for you. There are 100 of them, and some will speak to your experience more precisely than others. If you come to an idea that doesn't seem to fit you, simply ignore it and turn to another page.

Some of the 100 ideas will teach you about the basic principles of grief and mourning. One of the most important ways to help yourself is to learn about grief and mourning—what is myth and what is helpful. The remainder of the 100 ideas offer practical, here-and-now, action-oriented suggestions for embracing your grief and practicing self-compassion. Each idea is followed by a brief explanation of how and why the idea might help you.

You'll also notice that each of the 100 ideas offers a *carpe diem*, which means "seize the day." My hope is that you not relegate this book to your shelves but instead keep it handy on your nightstand or desk. Pick it up often and turn to any page; the carpe diem suggestion might help you seize the day by giving you an exercise, action, or thought to consider today, right now, right this minute.

While I do not believe in ranking losses in an attempt to define which kinds of losses are most painful and devastating to survivors, I have learned that both grieving parents and grieving grandparents have a particularly difficult journey ahead of them. The death of a child may indeed create life's greatest upheaval.

But remember, you are not alone, and your struggles are not forgotten. Millions of other grieving grandparents want you to know that you cannot only learn to survive, you can go on to discover renewal of meaning and purpose in your life. I am honored to pass along these resounding messages of hope and healing to you.

Finally, I have also discovered that no personal quality is more central to mourning the death of your grandchild than courage. Courage is the ability to do what one believes is right, even when others may strongly disagree. If people around you should try to persuade you to change the ways you are mourning the death of your grandchild, stay steadfast. As long as you are meeting your six needs of mourning (Ideas 10 through 15), trust your instincts.

I thank you from deep in my soul for having the courage to embrace the thoughts I've tried to express in this book. I hope we meet one day!

Alan D. Wolfelt

1.

GIVE YOURSELF
PERMISSION TO MOURN

*"What a bargain grandchildren are! I give them my loose change,
and they give me a million dollars' worth of pleasure."*
— Gene Perret

- You have experienced the loss of a grandchild. Your grief is very real. This death will affect you physically, emotionally, socially, intellectually, and spiritually.

- Sometimes grandparents set aside or discount their own grief because they are so focused on worrying about and supporting their grieving child (the grandchild's parent). Yes, your child very much needs and deserves your love and support right now. But *you* also need love and support.

- If you had a relationship with the grandchild who died, you will grieve. If your relationship was close, your grief will likely be profound and everlasting. If your relationship was not close, you may grieve the relationship you wish you could have had and regret the fact that it is now too late.

- No matter how old we are, no matter how many friends and family members die over the course of our lives, we grieve. Each time, our grief is as unique as the person who died and our relationship with him. Just because we are older does not mean we are "used" to death and take it in stride without being affected by it.

CARPE DIEM
Place a framed photo of your grandchild on your nightstand or
somewhere you will see it first thing when you wake up and last thing
before you go to sleep. Tell him how much you miss him.

2.

UNDERSTAND THE DIFFERENCE BETWEEN GRIEF AND MOURNING

"What happens when people open their hearts? They get better."
— Haruki Murakami

- Grief is the constellation of internal thoughts and feelings we have when someone we love dies. Grief is the weight in the chest, the churning in the gut, the unspeakable thoughts and feelings.

- Mourning is the outward expression of our grief. Mourning is crying, journaling, creating artwork, talking to others about the death, telling the story, speaking the unspeakable.

- Here's a way to remember which is which: The "i" in grief stands for what I feel inside. The "u" in mourn reminds me to share my grief with you.

- Everyone grieves when someone loved dies, but if we are to heal, we must also mourn.

- Many of the ideas in this book are intended to help you mourn the death of your grandchild, to express your grief outside of yourself. Over time, and with the support of others, to mourn is to heal.

CARPE DIEM:
Ask yourself this: Have I truly been mourning the death of my grandchild, or have I restricted myself to grieving?

3.

REMEMBER THAT LOVE NEVER ENDS

"Death ends a life, not a relationship."
— Mitch Albom

• You are probably old and wise enough by now to have learned that love never ends.

• Do you love your grandchild any less today than you did before his death? Of course not! Your love for your child and your grandchild (and theirs for you) will go on. I believe that they will go on forever. What do you believe?

• Your relationship with your grandchild will go on, too, but it will shift from a relationship of presence to a relationship of memory. If you believe in an afterlife, you may know that your relationship of presence, which has been paused for the time being, will continue after death.

• If this was your only grandchild or your child's only child, you may struggle with labels. It's normal and necessary to think and feel this issue through for yourself, but rest assured, you are still a grandparent, and your child is still a parent.

CARPE DIEM
Some people continue to foster a relationship of presence with a loved one who has died by talking to the person's photo, writing him letters, connecting with his spirit in places of special significance, etc. If this seems helpful and healing to you, give it a try today.

4.

ALLOW FOR NUMBNESS

*"There is a feeling of disbelief that comes over you, that takes over,
and you kind of go through the motions. You do what you're
supposed to do, but in fact you're not there at all."*
— Frederick Barthelme

- Feelings of shock, numbness, and disbelief are nature's way of temporarily protecting us from the full reality of the death of someone we love. Like anesthesia, these feelings help us survive the pain of our early grief. Be thankful for numbness.

- We often think, "I will wake up and this will not have happened." Early mourning can feel like being in a dream. Your emotions will need time to catch up with what your mind has been told.

- For grieving grandparents, feelings of helplessness may go hand-in-hand with numbness. At the same time you are in disbelief, you may also wish you could make it all go away—yet know that you can't.

- Even after you have moved beyond these initial feelings, don't be surprised if they re-emerge. Birthdays, holidays, and anniversaries often trigger these normal and necessary feelings. At times, feelings of shock and numbness may resurface for no apparent reason.

CARPE DIEM
If you're feeling numb, cancel any commitments that require
concentration and decision-making. Allow yourself time to regroup.
Find a "safe haven" that you might be able to retreat to for a few days.

5.

BE COMPASSIONATE WITH YOURSELF

*"Life Lesson 3: You can't rush grief. It has its own timetable.
All you can do is make sure there are lots of soft places
around—beds, pillows, arms, laps."*
— Patti Davis

- The journey through grief is a long and difficult one, especially for parents and grandparents who have suffered the death of a child. This death is wrong—it is unnatural; it is out of order; it is unfair; it is unfathomable.

- Be compassionate with yourself as you encounter painful thoughts and feelings. Allow yourself to think and do whatever you need to think and do to survive.

- Don't judge yourself or try to set a particular course for healing. There is no single, right way to grieve, and there is no timetable.

- Let your journey be what it is. And let yourself—your new, grieving self—be who you are.

- If others judge you or try to direct your grief in ways that seem hurtful or inappropriate, ignore them. You are the only expert of your grief. Usually such people are well-intentioned, but they lack insight. See if you can muster some compassion for them, too.

CARPE DIEM

What are you beating yourself up about these days? If you have the energy (and you won't always), address the problem head-on. If you can do something about it, do it. If you can't, try to be self-forgiving.

6.

BE COMPASSIONATE WITH YOUR CHILDREN, YOUR SPOUSE, AND ALL THE FAMILY MEMBERS GRIEVING THIS DEATH

"Each of us has his own rhythm of suffering."
— Roland Barthes

• Others are also deeply grieving this untimely death. Be as compassionate and nonjudgmental as you can be about their grief and behavior in the coming weeks and months. Give each other permission to mourn differently.

• Grieving family members are often not able to support one another well, especially in the early days of grief. They are simply too overcome with their own thoughts and feelings to be truly helpful to someone else. This is normal and not a failure of relationships within the family.

• Mothers (and grandmothers) sometimes feel that they are more affected by the death of a child. In fact, some research has shown that a mother's grief can be more disabling and longer lasting. Yet the intensity of feeling often depends most on each person's closeness to the child who died, not on gender. Fathers (and grandfathers) often feel the same depths of grief when a child dies, though these feelings are sometimes not expressed.

• Largely due to societal norms and expectations, men and women tend to mourn differently. Men often appear to be more stoic, and they may want to return to work faster. Women are typically more outwardly emotional and slower to return to daily routines. Yet in some families, these roles seem to be reversed. All these responses are normal and are not a gauge of each person's love for the child who died.

CARPE DIEM

Today, plan a time to talk to your partner or another family member about any unreconciled feelings you have toward him or her regarding the death, even if the death happened some time ago.
Your goal is not to accuse or judge but rather to listen and to love.

7.

BE COMPASSIONATE WITH YOUR SURVIVING GRANDCHILDREN

"A grandparent is a parent who has a second chance."
— Author unknown

- Grieving siblings are often "forgotten mourners." This means that their parents and family as well as friends and society tend to either overlook their ongoing grief or attempt to soothe it away.

- What grieving siblings and cousins really need is for adults to be open and honest with them about the death. And they need to know that their grief is important, too, and that their unique thoughts and feelings are acknowledged.

- Share your grief with your surviving grandchildren and make time to understand theirs. The parents of the child who died may understandably be too overwhelmed by their own grief to focus on their remaining children. As a grandparent, now is the time to step in and help your surviving grandkids feel safe, heard, and loved.

- Sometimes siblings of a child who died are put in the position of trying to parent their grieving mother and father. Yet children need to be children. They are not developmentally mature enough to act as caregivers, and they also need caregivers to focus on their grief. If you see this kind of role-reversal happening in your family, I encourage you to share in the parenting responsibilities and caregiving in order to relieve and support the children.

CARPE DIEM
Take your surviving grandchildren out to lunch or to the park and spend some time talking about their feelings since the death.
Find out if they are at risk of becoming "forgotten mourners."
If they are, spearhead a plan to get them the support they need.

8.

BE AWARE THAT YOUR GRIEF AFFECTS YOUR BODY, HEART, SOCIAL SELF, MIND, AND SPIRIT

"Grief is hard on friendships, but it doesn't have to be. Sometimes, all it takes is a little honesty between friends. If we gently and lovingly explain what we need from the relationship during our time of grief, and what we are willing to do in return, we can turn even a lukewarm friendship into something special."

— Margaret Brownley

- Grief is physically demanding. The body responds to the stress of the encounter and the immune system can weaken. You may be more susceptible to illness and physical discomforts. Grieving grandparents often describe their grief as a pain in the chest or a physical ache. You will probably also feel sluggish or highly fatigued. Some people call this the "lethargy of grief."

- The emotional toll of grief is complex and painful. Mourners often feel many different feelings, and those feelings can shift and blur over time.

- Bereavement naturally results in social discomfort. Friends and family often withdraw from mourners, leaving them isolated and unsupported. Mourners often feel out of place in a setting they once felt a part of.

- It's very common for mourners to be unable to concentrate and think clearly. If, like me, you normally experience your share of "senior moments," don't be surprised to find yourself even more cognitively affected in grief.

- Mourners often ask, "Why go on living?" "Will my life have meaning now?" "Where is God in this?" Spiritual questions such as these are natural and necessary but also draining.

- All five facets of your self are under attack. You may feel weak and powerless, especially in the early weeks and months. Only over time and through active mourning will you gain the strength to re-emerge as a new, whole you.

CARPE DIEM
If you've felt physically affected by your grief, see a doctor this week. Sometimes it's comforting to receive a clean bill of health.

9.

EXPECT TO HAVE A MULTITUDE OF FEELINGS

"No one ever told me that grief felt so like fear."
— C.S. Lewis

- Grieving grandparents don't just feel sad. They often feel numb, angry, guilty, afraid, regretful, confused, even relieved (in cases of chronic or terminal illness, for example). Sometimes these feelings follow each other within a short period of time, or they may occur simultaneously. I often say that grief is not experienced as a single note but as a chord.

- As strange as some of these emotions may seem to you, they are normal and healthy. At times, you may feel like you're "going crazy." Rest assured that you aren't going crazy: you're grieving.

- Allow yourself to feel whatever it is you are feeling without judging yourself.

- Talk about your feelings with someone who cares and can supportively listen.

CARPE DIEM
Which grief feeling has surprised you most? Make a point of talking about this feeling with someone today.

10.

UNDERSTAND THE SIX NEEDS OF MOURNING

Need #1: Acknowledge the reality of the death

"When you are born, you cry, and the world rejoices.
When you die, you rejoice, and the world cries."
— Buddhist saying

- Your grandchild has died. This is one of the most difficult realities in the world to accept. Yet gently, slowly, and patiently, you must embrace this reality, bit by bit, day by day.

- Whether your grandchild's death was sudden or anticipated, fully acknowledging the reality of the loss may take weeks, months, even years.

- You will first acknowledge the reality of the death with your head. Only over time will you come to acknowledge it with your heart.

- At times you may push away the reality of the death. This is normal and necessary for your survival. You will come to integrate the reality in doses as you are ready.

CARPE DIEM
Tell someone who doesn't know what happened about your grandchild today. Talking about both the life and the death will help you work on this important need.

11.

UNDERSTAND THE SIX NEEDS OF MOURNING

Need #2: Embrace the pain of the loss

"In the godforsaken, obscene quicksand of life, there is a deafening alleluia rising from the souls of those who weep, and of those who weep with those who weep. If you watch, you will see the hand of God putting the stars back in their skies one by one."

— Ann Weems

- This need requires mourners to embrace the pain of their loss—something we naturally don't want to do. It is easier to avoid, repress, or push away the pain of grief than it is to confront it.

- It is in embracing your grief, however, that you will learn to reconcile yourself to it.

- In the early days after the death of your grandchild, your pain may seem ever-present. Your every thought and feeling, every moment of every day, may seem painful. During this time, you will probably need to seek refuge from your pain. Go for a walk, read a book, watch TV, talk to supportive friends and family about the normal things of everyday life.

- While you do need to embrace the pain of your loss, you must do it in doses, over time. You simply cannot take in the enormity of your loss all at once. It's healthy to seek distractions and allow yourself bits of pleasure each day.

CARPE DIEM

If you feel up to it, allow yourself a time for embracing pain today. Dedicate 15 minutes to thinking about and feeling the loss. Reach out to someone who doesn't try to take your pain away and spend some time with him.

12.

UNDERSTAND THE SIX NEEDS OF MOURNING

Need #3: Remember the child who died

*"Some are bound to die young. By dying young a person
stays young in people's memory. If he burns brightly
before he dies, his brightness shines for all time."*
— Author unknown

- When someone we love dies, they live on in us through memory. Those of us who have lived a number of decades in this world know this well.

- To heal, grandparents and all family members need to actively remember the child who died and commemorate the life that was lived.

- Never let anyone take your memories away in a misguided attempt to save you from pain. It's good for you to continue to display photos of your grandchild. It's good to talk about memories, both happy and sad. It's good to cherish toys and other items that belonged to your grandchild.

- If you are grieving after a miscarriage or stillbirth, this need will focus on remembering your hoped-for expectations and dreams of the future.

- In the early weeks and months of your grief, you may fear that you will forget your grandchild—the details of her face, the tone of his voice, the special lilt in her walk. Rest assured that while time may blur some of your memories, as you slowly shift your relationship from one of presence to one of memory, you will indeed remember.

- Remembering the past makes hoping for the future possible.

CARPE DIEM
You might find it helpful to begin to write down memories of your grandchild. This is both a healing exercise and a way to hold on to special memories forever. Today, write down at least one memory.

13.

UNDERSTAND THE SIX NEEDS OF MOURNING

Need #4: Develop a new self-identity

"We define our identity always in dialogue with, sometimes in struggle against, the things our significant others want to see in us. Even after we outgrow some of these others—our parents, for instance—and they disappear from our lives, the conversation with them continues within us as long as we live."
— Charles Taylor

- In life, a big part of our self-identities is formed by the relationships we have with others, especially our family members. We are husbands and wives, parents and grandparents, children and siblings.

- You have gone from being a grandparent to a "bereaved grandparent." You thought of yourself, at least in part, as this unique child's grandmother or grandfather. Even if you have other grandchildren, this perception of yourself has changed. If the child who died was your only grandchild, you may wonder whether you are still a grandparent at all.

- While you must work through this difficult need yourself, I can assure you that you are and always will be your child's grandparent, for to become a grandparent is to walk through a door that can never be closed.

- Still, the way you defined yourself and the way society defines you is changed. You need to re-anchor yourself, to reconstruct your self-identity. This is arduous and painful work.

CARPE DIEM

Write out a response to this prompt: I used to be _____.
Now that _____ died, I am _____. This makes me feel
_____. Keep writing as long as you want.

14.

UNDERSTAND THE SIX NEEDS OF MOURNING

Need #5: Search for meaning

"I do not want the peace which passeth understanding.
I want the understanding which bringeth peace."
— Helen Keller

- When someone loved dies, we naturally question the meaning and purpose of life and death. When a child dies before a parent and a grandparent, these kinds of questions are particularly painful. Why should a child ever die before his grandparents? This death violates nature and the order of the universe.

- "Why" questions may surface uncontrollably and often precede "How" questions. "Why did this happen?" comes before "How will I go on living?"

- You will almost certainly question your philosophy of life and explore religious and spiritual values as you work on this need.

- Remember that having faith or spirituality does not negate your need to mourn. If you believe in an afterlife of some kind, your grandchild has still lost precious time on Earth, and you have lost time with him, too. It's normal to feel dumbfounded and angry at a God whom you may feel has permitted such a thing to happen.

- Ultimately, you may decide that there is no answer to the question "Why did this happen?" The death does not make sense. It never will.

CARPE DIEM

Write down a list of "why" questions that have surfaced for you since the death. Find a friend or counselor who will explore these questions with you without thinking she has to give you answers.

15.

UNDERSTAND THE SIX NEEDS
OF MOURNING

Need #6: Receive ongoing support from others

"If I can see pain in your eyes, then share with me your tears.
If I can see joy in your eyes, then share with me your smile."
— Santosh Kalwar

- As mourners, we need the love and understanding of others if we are to heal.

- Don't feel ashamed by your heightened dependence on others right now. If the death was recent, you may feel the need to be around people all the time. You may need to talk about the death often. You may need help running errands, doing laundry, or paying bills. Don't feel bad about this. Instead, take comfort in the knowledge that others care about you.

- Unfortunately, our society places too much value on "carrying on" and "doing well" after a death. So, many mourners are abandoned by their friends and family soon after the death. If the death of your grandchild was long ago, you may have experienced this abandonment firsthand. Keep in mind the rule of thirds: one-third of your friends will be supportive of your need to mourn; one-third will make you feel worse; and one-third will neither help nor hinder.

- Grief is experienced in "doses" over years, not quickly and efficiently, and you will need the continued support of your friends and family for weeks, months, and years. If you are not getting this support, ask for it. Usually people are more than willing to help—they just don't have any idea what to do (and what not to do).

CARPE DIEM
Sometimes your friends want to support you but don't know how.
Ask! Call your closest friend right now and tell him you need
his help through the coming weeks and months.

16.

KNOW THAT GRIEF DOES NOT PROCEED IN ORDERLY, PREDICTABLE "STAGES"

"The risk of love is loss, and the price of loss is grief. But the pain of grief is only a shadow when compared with the pain of never risking love."
— Hilary Stanton Zunin

- Though the "needs of mourning" (Ideas 10-15) are numbered 1-6, grief is not an orderly progression towards healing. Don't fall into the trap of thinking your grief journey will be predictable or always forward-moving. Mourning is really a "dosed" process of re-adapting to life with loss, and it continues throughout our lives.

- Usually, grief hurts more before it hurts less.

- You will probably experience a multitude of different emotions in a wave-like fashion. You will also likely encounter more than one need of mourning at the same time.

- Be compassionate with yourself as you experience your own unique grief journey.

CARPE DIEM

Has anyone told you that you are in this or that "stage" of grief?
Ignore this usually well-intentioned advice.
Don't allow yourself or anyone else to compartmentalize your grief.

17.

TAKE AN INVENTORY

*"Where you used to be, there is a hole in the world, which
I find myself constantly walking around in the daytime,
and falling in at night. I miss you like hell."*

— Edna St. Vincent Millay

- When your beautiful grandchild died, you lost not only her physical presence but so much more.
- You lost your hopes and dreams for her future as well as your family's future.
- You lost your commitment to always make things better for your child.
- You lost a part of yourself.
- You may have lost future great-grandchildren.
- You may have lost some of your faith in God.
- You may have lost your trust in medicine or your faith in the goodness of others.
- You may have lost your sense of how life is supposed to work.
- It's no wonder that your grief feels so, so heavy.

CARPE DIEM

Today, take an inventory of all you have lost as a result of this death.
Write it down and/or talk about it with someone who's a good listener.

18.

TAKE GOOD CARE OF YOURSELF

"The death of a beloved is an amputation."
— C.S. Lewis

- Good self-care is nurturing and necessary for mourners, yet it's something many of us completely overlook.

- Try very hard to eat well and get adequate rest. Lay your body down two to three times a day for 20-30 minutes, even if you don't sleep. I know—you probably don't care very much about eating well right now, and you may be sleeping poorly. But taking care of yourself is truly one way to fuel healing and to begin to embrace life again. It's also a way to ensure that you're well enough to support your grieving child.

- Drink at least five to six glasses of water each day. Dehydration can compound feelings of fatigue and disorientation.

- Exercise not only provides you with more energy, it can give you focused thinking time. Take a 20-minute walk every day. Or, if that seems too much, a five-minute walk. But don't over-exercise, because your body needs extra rest, as well.

- Now more than ever, you need to allow time for you.

CARPE DIEM
Are you taking a multi-vitamin?
If not, now is probably a good time to start.

19.

LET GO OF DESTRUCTIVE MYTHS ABOUT GRIEF AND MOURNING

*"They say time heals all wounds, but that presumes
the source of the grief is finite."*
— Cassandra Clare

- Like many of us, you have probably internalized many of our society's harmful myths about grief and mourning.

- Here are some to let go of:
    - I need to be strong and carry on.
    - I need to be strong for my child's sake.
    - Tears are a sign of weakness.
    - I need to get over my grief.
    - Death is something we don't talk about.
    - My grandchild wouldn't want me to be sad.

- Sometimes these myths will cause you to feel guilty about or ashamed of your true thoughts and feelings. They can also cause you to model unhealthy grieving behaviors for your family.

- Your grief is your grief. It's normal and necessary.
Allow it to be what it is.

CARPE DIEM
Which grief myth have you encountered most since the death?
Write about it in a journal.

20.

HELP YOUR CHILD...

"In times of grief and sorrow I will hold you and rock you and take your grief and make it my own. When you cry I cry and when you hurt I hurt. And together we will try to hold back the floods to tears and despair and make it through the potholed street of life."

— Nicholas Sparks

- As parents, our first and most powerful instinct is often to help our hurting child. Yes, by all means, be there to help your grieving child as much as you can in the coming weeks and months.

- You can help in many ways. You can listen. You can help with tasks and chores. You can hug and hold. You can listen some more.

- You can't take away your child's pain (and you shouldn't try to). But you can bear witness to her pain. You can be a loving, steadfast presence.

- Don't try to hide your own grief as she expresses hers. But when your own grief gets too overwhelming or you become fatigued from being a caregiver in grief, you'll need to take a break. Retreat, rest, and replenish, then return. If it seems appropriate, arrange for someone else to help support your child while you take a much-needed respite.

CARPE DIEM

When your child was a baby, did you have help caring for her? Did you and your spouse share caregiving duties? Maybe you can share again now. Did others help you sometimes, such as grandparents, neighbors, or cousins? Call in others to help now too.

21.

...AND GET HELP FOR YOURSELF

"Too often we underestimate the power of a touch, a smile, a kind word, a listening ear, an honest compliment, or the smallest act of caring, all of which have the potential to turn a life around."

— Leo Buscaglia

- Yes, you must help your child, but you are also grieving the death of your grandchild at the same time that you are grieving the grief suffered by your child. You also need help and love and support.

- Naturally, your grieving child may not be able to support you during this difficult time. Not only are you the caregiver and he the child in your relationship, but his normal and necessary grief may well prevent him from reciprocating your care even a little.

- Many others in your extended family may also be focusing on their own grief and unable to support you. So, you may need to reach outside the family for help.

- Turn to your friends. The support of even one loyal friend over the coming months may be enough to sustain you.

- I would also encourage you to consider a support group and/or grief counseling. Both are excellent self-care measures that will not only help you heal, they will also make you more able to help your child when he needs you.

CARPE DIEM

Identify at least one—and preferably two or three—people you can turn to when you need to express your grief. Contact one of them today.

22.

CREATE A SACRED SPACE
IN YOUR HOME

*"Sometimes a reminder of life's blessings hanging in our
home is all that's needed to console a grieving heart."*
— Author unknown

- Your grandchild occupied a special place in your heart—a place that no one else will ever fill. It is in this place that your memories and love for this child still live.

- You can honor your grandchild and help yourself mourn in healthy ways by creating a special place in your home in her memory.

- After my father died, I placed photos of him, alone and with friends and family, in a place where I would see them often. I surrounded the photos with linking objects (see Idea 32) that connected me to him, such as his tennis racket and a favorite baseball cap. This became a sacred place where I could stop and mourn, remember, share my memories with others, and heal.

- Sometimes people think this practice is morbid or wrong. They may judge that you've created a "shrine," when in fact you've created a sacred space to give honor to someone who will forever be in your heart. As long as it is helping you embrace your feelings and memories and also express them outside of yourself, creating a sacred space in your home is healthy and will help you heal.

CARPE DIEM
Today, create a special place in your home to honor the life and
death of your grandchild. You might place photos, shadow boxes,
and memorabilia in this spot. Consider locating it in or near your
main living area so that it gives you the opportunity to share it and talk
about it with others. You will discover who will support you in your grief
and who cannot depending on how they perceive your sacred space.

23.

USE YOUR GRANDCHILD'S NAME

"My grandchild has taught me what true love means. It means watching Scooby-Doo cartoons while the basketball game is on another channel."
— Gene Perret

- When you're talking about your family—or about your life in general, don't avoid using the name of the child who died. Though it is bittersweet to say and to hear, actively remembering those who have died is one of the six central needs of mourning.

- Sometimes others are afraid to use the name in your presence, out of fear that it is painful to you. But if you use the name, they will know that they can use it, too.

- Acknowledge the significance of the death by talking about the child: "I remember when David…," "I was thinking of Sarah today because…," "Jordan always loved your pecan pie…"

- Ask your friends and family to use your grandchild's name, too. Grieving parents and grandparents often love to hear that special name.

CARPE DIEM
Today, say your grandchild's name out loud in a
conversation with someone.

24.

TELL THE STORY, OVER AND OVER AGAIN IF YOU FEEL THE NEED

"I know now that we never get over great losses; we absorb them, and they carve us into different, often kinder, creatures. We tell the story to get them back, to capture the traces of footfalls through the snow."

— Gail Caldwell

- Acknowledging a death is a painful, ongoing task that we accomplish in doses, over time. A vital part of healing in grief is often "telling the story" over and over again. It's as if each time you tell the story, it becomes a little more real.

- The "story" relates the circumstances surrounding the death of the child, reviewing the relationship you had with the child, describing aspects of the personality of the child who died, and sharing memories, good and bad.

- Grieving parents and grandparents can almost always recount in vivid and very specific detail what the day of the death was like for them.

- Find people who are willing to listen to you tell your story, over and over again if necessary, without judgment.

- You and your spouse or other family members may find great comfort in telling each other stories and sharing memories of the child's life. Ask your spouse to tell you the story of the time when…

CARPE DIEM

Tell the story of your grandchild's life and death to someone today in the form of a letter. Perhaps you can write and send this letter to a friend who lives far away.

25.

BE A GOOD LISTENER

*"Give sorrow words; the grief that does not speak whispers
the o'er-fraught heart and bids it break."*
— William Shakespeare

- Your child is hurting. While you can't take her pain away, you can listen as she shares her painful thoughts and feelings.

- Being a good listener to someone in deep grief is hard. When that someone is your child, whom you want to soothe, for whom you would rather kiss the pain away, it is especially hard.

- Being a good listener to someone in grief means listening without judging or trying to take her feelings away. It means empathizing and being present to the pain. It does not mean trying to fix things, give easy answers, or stop the tears.

- Lean in, make eye contact, offer touch when appropriate, and listen.

- Because you are grieving too, you will probably have to listen in doses. Listen, then retreat and recuperate before listening again. Find someone who will listen to you as you mourn and decompress.

CARPE DIEM

Today, try to be a good listener to someone who is grieving this death.

26.

DON'T SAY THIS

"Attempting to get at truth means rejecting stereotypes and clichés."
— Harold Evans

- You naturally want to comfort and soothe your child who is grieving. In a well-intentioned (but misguided) effort to take his pain away, you may find yourself falling back on platitudes, such as

  - I know how you feel.

  - _____ wouldn't want you to cry or be sad.

  - You have other children, and they need you.
    (Or, You can have another child.)

  - We should be happy we had her as long as we did.

  - If the child was sick: It's probably a blessing/for the best.

  - Now you have an angel in heaven.

  - Time heals all wounds.

  - It's all part of God's plan.

- Simple clichés such as these take away the griever's right to feel complicated combinations of sad, angry, hurt, and other emotions.

CARPE DIEM
Perhaps others have said such things to you since the death of your precious grandchild. Consider how it made you feel.

27.

SAY THIS INSTEAD

"Never underestimate the power of the words 'I love you' or the comfort of a simple hug. Grow your love daily."
— Elizabeth Bourgeret

- I'm so, so sorry.
- I love you.
- I'm here for you. I will always be here for you.
- I miss _____ too. I love her so much.
- I know I can't take the pain away. But I want to help. Please let me help by _____.
- You are a (good, loving, attentive, whatever adjective fits) parent. (Elaborate with examples.)
- I'm proud of you.
- Please, tell me what you are thinking and feeling. I will listen.

CARPE DIEM
Write your grieving child a note today and send it to her in the mail. Share with her what is on your heart.

28.

LEARN ABOUT THE COMPASSIONATE FRIENDS

*"Grandchildren are the dots that connect the lines
from generation to generation."*
— Lois Wyse

- The Compassionate Friends is the largest organization of grieving parents, siblings, and grandparents in the United States. Its chapters hold support groups and events in hundreds of communities. Visit them on the web at www.compassionatefriends.org. Bereaved Parents of the U.S.A. (www.bereavedparentsusa.org) is another growing and reputable organization that supports not only parents but grieving siblings and grandparents as well.

- The Compassionate Friends' credo begins, "We need not walk alone. We reach out to each other with love, with understanding, and with hope." (Visit their website to read the entire statement.) Reaching out to others and accepting their help is one of the six needs of mourning (see Idea 15).

- In addition to visiting the website and attending local chapter meetings, the national office also staffs a toll-free phone line. Call 877-969-0010 or email nationaloffice@compassionatefriends.org. A friendly staff member or volunteer will help you.

CARPE DIEM

Today, try using the Compassionate Friends' chapter locater tool, which you'll find on their website. Find the chapter nearest you and take note of when their next meeting is. Call or e-mail the chapter if you have questions. Some chapters actually have specific programs and resources to support grandparents. Consider attending the next meeting.

29.

IF YOU FEEL HELPLESS, TALK ABOUT IT

*"Grief is a most peculiar thing; we're so helpless in the face of it.
It's like a window that will simply open of its own accord.
The room grows cold, and we can do nothing but shiver."*
— Arthur Golden

- Many grieving grandparents have told me how helpless they feel—helpless to change or do anything about what happened, helpless to make their own child feel better.

- As parents, our instinct when our children are hurt is to "make it all better." Oh how you may wish you could make this all better. This is a normal feeling, one that grew out of our evolutionary demands as parents to protect our offspring.

- Helplessness is a horrible feeling. It means, in essence, that you want to help—that your heart and soul are crying out for you to help—but in reality there's nothing you can do to make it all better.

- If you feel helpless since the death, talk to someone about your thoughts and feelings. Sharing your most powerful, prominent inside feelings outside of yourself takes away some of their power. Mourning eases what's inside you.

CARPE DIEM
Today, talk to someone about your feelings of helplessness.
After this conversation, notice if your sense of powerlessness
has softened, if only a tiny little bit.

30.

IF YOU FEEL GUILTY, TALK ABOUT IT

"The bitterest tears shed over graves are for words left unsaid and deeds left undone."
— Harriet Beecher Stowe

- Grieving grandparents often feel guilty because, as we explored in the Introduction, they outlived their grandchild. This death was out of order. They should be the ones who died—not the grandchild.

- Sometimes after a death, feelings of guilt stem from "I should have…" or "I wish I would have…" thoughts. If we could go back and change a sequence of events, perhaps the death could have been prevented. These kinds of "if only" thoughts are normal, even if, as is usually the case, no one is really "at fault."

- Feelings of guilt, regret, and remorse are common in grief. This doesn't mean that you or anyone who loved the child who died did anything wrong. It just means that it's human nature to look for fault. It's simply part of our wiring as we try to understand and come to terms with what happened.

- As with all feelings in grief, guilt is neither good nor bad, right nor wrong. It simply is. And it needs to be expressed in order to be worked through.

CARPE DIEM
If you have been keeping feelings of guilt, regret, or remorse inside, share them with someone else today. As long as they reside in you, that means you need to keep expressing them.

31.

IF YOU FEEL ANGRY, TALK ABOUT IT

"Anger is a symptom, a way of cloaking and expressing feelings too awful to experience directly—hurt, bitterness, grief, and, most of all, fear."
— Joan Rivers

- Anger is a common and understandable response after the death of a young person.

- It's not fair! we think. Life isn't supposed to work this way! After a death, sometimes our anger gets directed at a certain person, such as a doctor, or entity, such as a carmaker (in cases where a car's safety equipment wasn't adequate). We can also feel angry with one another for what we perceive someone did or did not do that may have contributed to the death.

- Anger, rage, and blame are, at bottom, protest emotions. They are how we protest a reality that we wish were not true.

- As with all feelings in grief, anger is neither good nor bad, right nor wrong. It simply is. And it needs to be expressed in order to be worked through.

- With anger, it's important that its expression does not physically or emotionally hurt someone else (or even ourselves). Find more constructive ways to express anger, such as physical activity or talking with a friend or counselor.

CARPE DIEM
Are you angry about the death? If you are, share your angry thoughts and feelings with a neutral but compassionate friend today.

32.

UNDERSTAND THE ROLE OF "LINKING OBJECTS"

"In French you don't really say, 'I miss you.' You say Tu me manques, *which means, 'You are missing from me.'"*
— Author unknown

- Grieving grandparents are often comforted by physical objects associated with the child who died. It is not unusual to save favorite clothing, jewelry, toys, locks of hair, and other personal items.

- Such "linking objects" will help you remember your grandchild and honor the life that was lived. Such objects may help you heal.

- Never think that being attached to these objects is morbid or wrong. If someone tells you that you're crazy for displaying your grandson's sweatshirt or not washing the pillowcase your granddaughter used the last time she slept over, ignore them. You're not crazy; you're simply holding on to what you have left.

- Never hurry into disposing of your grandchild's belongings—and never force your child to do so, either. Your grandchild's parents may want to leave the child's bedroom untouched for months or sometimes years. This is OK as long as the objects offer comfort and don't inhibit healing.

CARPE DIEM
When and only when your child is ready, offer to help sort through your grandchild's belongings. Be sure to fill a memory box with significant objects and mementos.

33.

PAY ATTENTION TO YOUR BODY LANGUAGE

"The body never lies."
— Martha Graham

- About 60 to 80 percent of all communication comes not from what we say but how we hold and move our bodies when we talk to someone else. In other words, our body language (and tone of voice) say much more than the words we speak.

- Making eye contact when you are listening to or present to someone else is important. So is maintaining an open posture (not crossing your arms or legs) and leaning a bit forward, toward the other person.

- An open body posture says, "I'm here for you. I'm ready to receive what you would like to communicate."

- Also, don't multitask when you're listening to something important that someone else is trying to tell you. Put down your phone, empty your hands, face the person, and really listen.

CARPE DIEM

Talk to yourself in the mirror today. Try on different postures,
facial expressions, and tones of voice. Notice which make you
the most caring, empathetic communicator.

34.

TALK TO OTHER GRIEVING GRANDPARENTS

*"Nobody can do for little children what grandparents do.
Grandparents sort of sprinkle stardust over the lives of little children."*
— Alex Haley

- You are not alone. At any given moment, millions of other grandparents the world over live on after the death of a grandchild.

- I do not mean to diminish your unique pain. What matters to you, I understand, is not that countless grandchildren die every year but that *your* precious grandchild has died. It is not the same. It is never the same.

- Still, even though your grief is indeed your grief and no one else was quite like your grandchild, many other grieving grandparents have walked this lonely road. Reaching out to them, listening to them, and embracing their support and their messages of hope and healing will probably help make your grief journey more tolerable.

- If it turns out that you come into contact with several other grandparents who are grieving, you might consider creating an informal support group. Maybe you would like to meet for coffee and discussion once a week or once a month.

CARPE DIEM
Today, reach out to another grandparent whom you know to be grieving the death of a grandchild. If appropriate, consider reaching out to the grandparents on the other side of the grandchild's family.

35.

IF YOU ARE ALONE...

"Our language has wisely sensed the two sides of being alone. It has created the word 'loneliness' to express the pain of being alone. And it has created the word 'solitude' to express the glory of being alone."
— Paul Tillich

- Some grieving grandparents are widowed or divorced. They find themselves literally alone in their grief.

- If you are alone, I want you to read and reread Idea 15, the sixth need of mourning: Receive ongoing support from others.

- You will need to work especially hard to reach out to others in the coming months. Do not isolate yourself in your grief. Instead, spend time with your family and friends, join a support group (in person or online), connect with others at a senior center or your place of worship, and consider seeing a grief counselor.

- Remember this Swedish proverb: Shared joy is a double joy; shared sorrow is half a sorrow.

CARPE DIEM

If you are alone in your grief, please reach out to someone else today. Maybe there is someone else grieving this death who is also alone. If so, reach out to this person.

36.

FIND A GRIEF "BUDDY"

"I say find one true friend to help you get through the tough times."
— Kelly Osbourne

- Though no one else will grieve a death exactly as you are grieving the loss of your unique grandchild, other grieving grandparents have had similar experiences.

- Find a grief "buddy"—someone who is also in mourning the death of a grandchild, someone you can talk to, someone who also needs a companion in grief right now.

- Make a pact with your grief buddy to call each other whenever one of you needs to talk. Promise to listen without judgment. Commit to spending time together.

- You might arrange to meet once a week for breakfast or lunch with your grief buddy.

CARPE DIEM
Do you know another grieving grandparent who also needs grief support right now? Call her and ask her out to lunch today.
If it feels right, discuss the possibility of being grief buddies.

37.

OFFER PRACTICAL HELP

"We only have what we give."
— Isabel Allende

- After a grandchild dies, it is the grandparent's normal and natural instinct to want to help her child—the grandchild's mother or father. (Unless the grandparent and her child are estranged or have a difficult relationship.)

- But helping someone else mourn when you yourself are mourning can be hard. It's emotionally exhausting, especially when you know the grief journey will go on for years and years.

- Offer emotional support how and when you can, yes, but also offer practical help. Pitch in with errands, meals, and other chores. Help take care of the remaining grandchildren.

- You may be a natural helper, someone who steps in easily to do what needs doing. But if you're not a natural helper, try being one now. Step outside your comfort zone. Give of yourself. It will help everyone involved, including you.

CARPE DIEM
Do something that needs doing for your grandchild's immediate family or household without being asked.

38.

OFFER YOUR PRESENCE

*"To us, family means putting your arms
around each other and being there."*
— Barbara Bush

- Throughout life, there is no greater gift you can give than that of your presence. Perhaps you have learned that. I certainly have.

- Just being there to support your grieving child and the others who are grieving—and for them to support you in return—is often the best way you can help, especially in the early days and weeks after the death.

- Yes, everyone is busy, and yes, it can sometimes feel awkward or strange to spend a lot of time in your adult child's home (or he in yours), but there's no time like the present to change old habits and create new ways of being together.

- If your child rebuffs your offers to spend time with her, whether in her home or yours, don't be too pushy—but don't give up, either. Never stop trying to connect.

CARPE DIEM
If you live close, stop by to see your child today for no specific
reason. Offer to share a meal or watch a ballgame together.
If you live farther away, plan to travel to your child's home soon or,
if that's not possible, learn to Skype.

39.

ADOPT SOMEONE

"How wonderful that no one need wait a single moment to improve the world."

— Anne Frank

- Your heart has a hole that can never be filled by anyone else. This is true. Your grandchild was one-of-a-kind.

- But our hearts do have the capacity to expand infinitely. We can allow others in. We can make an effort to bring others in. Ongoing, vibrant relationships will not only help heal your grief, they are what make life worth living.

- Do you know someone who is lonely or in need of help? Adopt this person. Offer him your time and your kindness.

- A widowed neighbor, a single parent, a troubled teen. So many people out there would have much better lives if we shared of ourselves and gave them a little love, attention, and support.

CARPE DIEM
Who do you know who needs help of some kind?
Reach out to this person today.

40.

BE AWARE OF OTHER GRIEFS
YOU MAY BE CARRYING

"Everybody has their burdens, their grief that they carry with them."
— Elizabeth Edwards

- If you don't express your grief in life—that is, if you don't fully mourn it, you will continue to carry it inside you. Carried grief often results in problems with intimacy, depression, substance abuse, and other issues.

- By now you have surely experienced other significant losses in your life. None of us escapes grief. But have you mourned each loss along the way?

- Many of us were raised in families in which death was a taboo subject. Grief was something you didn't show or talk about. As a result, many, many older adults out there are carrying a great deal of unexpressed grief.

- As you do your grief work (and it is work!) of expressing your thoughts and feelings about the death of your precious grandchild, you will probably notice that older griefs are also bubbling up inside you. If you are carrying a lot of past grief, I encourage you to see a compassionate grief counselor who will help you work on what I call "catch-up mourning."

- Finally setting down your carried grief feels like unburdening your soul. It has the potential to transform your life and open you to love and joy in a way you never have experienced before.

CARPE DIEM
Talk to someone today about this idea of carried grief. Share your experiences with mourning—or not mourning—after past losses.

41.

WEAR A SYMBOL OF MOURNING

"I wear my heart on my sleeve."
— Princess Diana

- In centuries past, grieving women often made jewelry or wreaths out of locks of hair that belonged to a child who had died. Black clothing was required for a period of one year. Mourners wore black armbands.

- These symbols of mourning accorded a special status to mourners, saying, in effect, "Someone I love has died. Please offer me your respect and your condolences."

- Today, we no longer identify mourners in these ways, creating the harmful illusion that "everything's back to normal" even though it's not (and never will be).

- How do you let others know that you're still in mourning and still need their support? The best way is to tell them. Talk about the death and its continuing impact on your life. Let your friends and family know you still need their help.

CARPE DIEM
Make a symbol of mourning part of your everyday dress.
Some grandparents wear jewelry that belonged to the child who died.
You might fill a locket with a photo and a lock of hair or wear a photo
button on your jacket. Or make a black armband and wear it proudly.

42.

EXPRESS YOUR FAITH

"Never be afraid to trust an unknown future to a known God."
— Corrie ten Boom

- Above all, mourning is a spiritual journey of the heart and soul. The death of a young person gives rise to the most profound spiritual yearnings and chaos. It is important to begin to examine your beliefs about death and develop an understanding of where God is in your suffering.

- If you have faith or spirituality, express it in ways that seem appropriate to you.

- Attending church or your place of worship, reading religious texts, and praying are a few conventional ways of expressing your faith. Be open to less conventional ways, as well, such as meditating or spending time alone in nature.

- For many grieving grandparents, having faith means feeling sure that they will one day see their grandchild again. This belief alone, whether in heaven, through reincarnation, or in a less defined kind of afterlife, makes life bearable. Do you believe you will be reunited with your grandchild one day? If you do, allow yourself to revel in its comforts. Close your eyes and envision your concept of heaven. See your grandchild smiling at you, welcoming you, reaching out to hold you. Retreat to this image when you are sad or disheartened.

CARPE DIEM
Visit your place of worship today, either for services or
for an informal time of prayer and solitude.

43.

THINK YOUNG

"Youth is happy because it has the capacity to see beauty.
Anyone who keeps the ability to see beauty never grows old."
— Franz Kafka

- It is the nature of children to live for the moment and appreciate today. All of us would benefit from a little more childlike wonder.

- Do something childish—blow bubbles, swing on a swing, visit a toy store, build a sand castle, fly a kite, go for a bike ride.

- If you have other grandchildren (or great-grandchildren!), spend time with them. The death of a young person makes all of us aware of how precious each and every day is. Don't waste opportunities to be with your grandchildren and others you care about. Right now. Today.

- You can also spend time with children in other ways. Volunteer at a local school. Take a friend's children to the park one afternoon.

- What was your favorite activity as a kid? I liked to ride bike and play catch. Plan to give one of your old favorites another try today.

CARPE DIEM
Buy a gift for a child today just because.

44.

GIVE SOMETHING AWAY

*"You give but little when you give of your possessions.
It is when you give of yourself that you truly give."*
— Khalil Gibran

- It's easy to fall into the trap of clinging to belongings instead of relationships.

- I bet if you could, you'd trade any given day you spent shopping or cleaning or fixing with one more minute with your grandchild.

- Now might be a good time for you to pare down your belongings. You probably don't need most of them anyway, and maybe someone else would put them to good use. (Besides, it's not fair to expect your children to clean out your house when the time comes. You bought the stuff; you should deal with the stuff!)

- You can donate belongings to thrift stores. You can give special heirlooms to family members now, while you're still here to take pleasure in watching them be used.

CARPE DIEM
Every day for the next week, give at least one thing away. Start today by giving away something that is special but that you no longer use.

45.

ORGANIZE A MEMORY BOOK

*"So long as the memory of certain beloved friends lives in my heart,
I shall say that life is good."*
— Helen Keller

- Assembling a scrapbook that holds treasured photos and mementos of your grandchild can be a very healing activity.

- You might consider including her artwork, newspaper clippings, locks of hair, ticket stubs—anything you might have tucked into drawers that reminds you of her and the times you shared together.

- This activity can be just for you or for your whole family. You might be surprised how much your child and his family get into it once everyone gets started.

- Phone others who loved your grandchild and ask them to write a note for the scrapbook or contribute photos.

- Once it's finished, you might display the memory book on a special easel or stand in your family room.

- A similar but simpler idea is to place photos and mementos into a special box. Any time you're missing your grandchild, you can get out this memory box and spend a few minutes going through its contents.

CARPE DIEM
Buy an appropriate scrapbook or keepsake box today.
Don't forget to buy the associated materials you'll need, such as
photo pages or photo corners, glue, scissors, etc.

46.

MAKE A SHADOW BOX
OR MEMORY QUILT

*"Our lives are like quilts—bits and pieces,
joy and sorrow, stitched with love."*
— Author unknown

- Now, I realize that all grandparents are not crafty or quilters. (I'm not a grandparent quite yet, but when I do become one, I will not be quilting.) But whether you're good at it or not, making something physical that captures your memories of your grandchild is a healing process.

- Gather up photos and memorabilia that remind you of your grandchild. Buy an empty shadow box (a deep, glassed frame for displaying three-dimensional objects) at your local craft store and affix these items to the board. Lots of scrapbooking doodads are also available at craft stores and can help you capture the unique interests and personality of the child who died.

- A memory quilt made from scraps of clothing and blankets that belonged to the child who died is a powerfully touching and, ultimately, healing gift, either for yourself or for the parents or siblings of the child who died. Quilts can also be made of photos transferred to fabric. If you're not a quilter, you can find a number of seamstresses online who specialize in making custom memory quilts.

CARPE DIEM
If appropriate, offer to make (or have made) two memory
quilts that capture the life of your grandchild—
one for the child's parents (or sibling or spouse) and one for you.

47.

BE OPEN WITH YOUR CHILD

*"If you do not tell the truth about yourself,
you cannot tell it about other people."*
— Virginia Woolf

- Your child has suffered a terrible loss. You, too, have suffered a terrible loss. One way to help each other during this terrible time is with honesty.

- Be gentle but open. Tell your child what you are thinking and feeling. Cry in his presence if you feel like it. Encourage him to be open as well.

- If yours has historically been a family in which feelings are not shared and pain is buttoned up, try breaking free of that harmful habit now. It may seem awkward and scary at first, but you will soon see how honesty and openness, in small doses at least, create closer relationships and foster healing.

- Of course, I encourage you to employ compassion and tact. Now is not the time to blame or rage at your child, even if he did something wrong. If this is the case, use the principle of "tough love"—expressing your love and support at the same time you define healthy boundaries and ask him to take responsibility for his own actions.

CARPE DIEM
Try saying something both loving and honest to your child today.

48.

BE AWARE OF THE
PRESSURE COOKER PHENOMENON

"Laughter is the valve on the pressure cooker of life. Either you laugh and suffer, or you got your beans or brains on the ceiling."
— Wavy Gravy

- Everyone who was affected by this death is grieving. Each and every one of these people needs and deserves the empathetic understanding and support of others.

- But wait…how can this work? Everyone needs help at the same time!

- When a family has been affected by a death, you'll see what I call the "pressure cooker phenomenon." Typically everyone has a high need to feel understood yet a low capacity to be understanding.

- In the Introduction to this book, I talked about how grandparents are often "forgotten mourners." That is, their grief is not considered as significant or "important" as the grief of the child's parents or siblings (or spouse and children, if the grandchild was older and had a family of his own). Yet you know only too well that this is not true. Your own deep grief may well have you feeling the effects of the pressure cooker.

- If the pressure cooker phenomenon is making it hard for you to find support within your family, try turning to friends. Online forums comprised of others who have experienced the death of a grandchild can also be helpful.

- If you are seeing the pressure cooker phenomenon within your family, consider arranging a family meeting to talk about it.

CARPE DIEM
If you've ever used an old-fashioned pressure cooker (a kind of cooking pot where the lid clamps tight to the base, creating higher air pressure inside the pot), you know that there's a safety valve on the top that rocks back and forth to let off some steam. Without the safety valve, the pressure cooker would explode. Find a way today for you and other family members affected by the death to let off some steam.

49.

DRAW ON YOUR WISDOM

"Becoming a grandmother is wonderful. One moment you're just a mother. The next you are all-wise and prehistoric."
— Pam Brown

- It's true that with age comes wisdom.

- I don't know about you, but the older I get, the more I understand what's really important in life. I don't necessarily feel "wise" all the time, but I do think I have lessons and, yes, wisdom, to pass along to others, especially those younger than me.

- During your lifetime, you have probably seen and experienced a number of tragic losses. What helped you not only survive but grow after these experiences? How can you use this hard-won wisdom to help others who are grieving right now?

- If you're feeling more lost than wise right now, which would be perfectly understandable after the death of a grandchild, seek out the advice of someone your age or older whom you believe lives a life of openness, abundance, and love—despite having suffered.

CARPE DIEM
Consider sharing your wisdom in the form of a letter to the parents of the child who died. Don't offer clichés or platitudes, but do share your genuine stories, thoughts, and feelings.

50.

GO EASY ON PEOPLE
WHO SAY STUPID THINGS

*"Two things are infinite: the universe and human stupidity;
and I'm not sure about the universe."*
— Albert Einstein

- I'm sure you've realized by now that people don't know what to say to a grieving grandparent. Often they say the wrong things:
  - "Time heals all wounds."
  - "God wouldn't give you more than you can handle."
  - "At least you had her as long as you did."
  - "You have other grandchildren."
  - "Now you have an angel in heaven."
  - "You'll grow so much stronger because of this."
  - "I know how you feel."

- Most of these people are well-intentioned. They truly don't realize how phrases like these diminish your unique and significant loss. Perhaps instead of getting angry at them, you can keep in mind that they are, in fact, trying to help. How many hurtful things did you inadvertently say to mourners before your loss? As Maya Angelou wrote, "You did what you knew how to do, and when you knew better, you did better."

- Sometimes entering into an honest, deeper discussion with such people about what the death has really been like for you is a way to break through the clichés, helping them as well as you.

CARPE DIEM
Try talking with your partner (or a close friend) about the hurtful remarks others sometimes make. Say, "Aren't you disappointed when people say…" This conversation may help you express your feelings of hurt and frustration.

51.

LOOK INTO SUPPORT GROUPS

"Never doubt that a small group of thoughtful, committed citizens can change the world. Indeed, it's the only thing that ever has."
— Margaret Mead

- Grief support groups are a healing, safe place for many mourners to express their thoughts and feelings. Grieving grandparents may be able to find genuine understanding and comfort in support groups comprised of grieving parents and grandparents that they can't find anywhere else.

- Sharing similar experiences with other grieving families may help you feel like you're not alone, that you're not going crazy.

- Your local hospice or funeral home may offer a free or low-cost support group. The Compassionate Friends may also have a local chapter.

- If you are newly bereaved, you may not feel ready for a support group. Many mourners are more open to joining a support group six to nine months after the death. You will know when and if you feel ready to consider a support group.

- When to stop going to a support group is another question many grieving people have. Sometimes you just know it's time for you to graduate. Other times you may want to stay around to support more newly bereaved people. The only good answer to this question is whenever the group begins to feel less helpful, less relevant, or more of a burden than a help. Sometimes certain group members affect the group's dynamic in harmful ways. In this case, starting a new group is also an option.

CARPE DIEM

Call around today for support group information. If you're feeling ready, plan to attend a meeting this week or next.

52.

SEE A COUNSELOR

*"Our wounds are often the openings into the best
and most beautiful part of us."*
— David Richo

- While grief counseling is not for everyone, many grieving families are helped through their grief journeys by a compassionate counselor.

- If possible, find a counselor who has experience with grief and loss issues. Not all counselors are good at helping those who mourn. In fact, some are downright lousy at it. If you start seeing a counselor who doesn't seem to be helpful after several sessions, it's OK to move on to a different one.

- As with a support group, you may be more ready for counseling six months to a year after the death than you are immediately after. And it's never too late to see a counselor, even years after your grandchild's death.

- Ask your friends for referrals to a counselor who's helped them.

- A clergyperson may also be a good person to talk to during this time, but only if he affirms your need to mourn this death and search for meaning. Believing in God and an afterlife does not mean you shouldn't mourn!

CARPE DIEM
Schedule an initial interview with at least two counselors so
you can see whom you're most comfortable with.

53.

GET TO KNOW YOUR GRANDCHILD

"If I had known how wonderful it would be to have grandchildren, I'd have had them first."

— Lois Wyse

- Maybe you didn't know your grandchild as well as you wish you had…and now it's too late. That's a heavy burden to carry. Of course, in today's families, distance often hampers our ability to build a relationship.

- It's really not too late, though. You can still get to know your grandchild better by talking with people who were close to her.

- If appropriate, tell your child that you're feeling sad and remorseful that you didn't spend more time with the grandchild. Then ask your child to tell you everything he can about his precious child who died. This conversation may be filled with tears but also laughter. Be open and compassionate with one another as you talk.

- You can also talk to your grandchild's friends, teachers, and coaches. You can read her Facebook page. (Ask for help if you don't know how.) Whatever efforts you make to get to know your grandchild will be time well spent.

CARPE DIEM
Today, make it a point to learn at least one thing about
your grandchild that you didn't know.

54.

BEFRIEND THE
OTHER GRANDPARENTS

"What children need most are the essentials that grandparents provide in abundance. They give unconditional love, kindness, patience, humor, comfort, lessons in life. And, most importantly, cookies."
— Rudy Giuliani

- It's almost certain that you aren't the only grandparent or great-grandparent grieving this death.

- In addition to your spouse or partner, on the other side of the grandchild's family are other devastated grandparents. In some divorced and blended families, there are multiple sets of grandparents. Other families have "honorary" grandparents—that is, neighbors or friends of the family who are very close to the children and have acted in the capacity of grandparent.

- Consider reaching out to some or all of the other grandparents. You share a profound loss, and you can help one another now. Even if you didn't know the other grandparents well before the death, you can get to know them now.

CARPE DIEM
Today, write a note to or call one of the other grandparents.
Share your thoughts and feelings about the death
and express your compassion for theirs.

55.

GIVE TO THE CAUSE

"Happiness exists on earth, and it is won through prudent exercise of reason, knowledge of the harmony of the universe, and constant practice of generosity."
— Jose Marti

• Financial giving is not only a way of supporting a cause, it's a way to affirm to yourself what you believe is important.

• "Putting your money where your mouth is" is a kind of ritual, really. It's a physical act that gives concrete, practical shape to your passions and values.

• Is there a nonprofit working to prevent the illness or type of event that caused your grandchild's death? Consider supporting them with a financial gift in your grandchild's name. Alternately, you might choose to support a cause that was near and dear to your grandchild's heart.

• How much you are able to give is less important than the act of giving. Every dollar makes a difference.

CARPE DIEM
What cause or activity do you most associate with your grandchild's life or death? Mail a check or make an online donation today.

56.

KEEP A JOURNAL

"When I go back and read my journals or fiction, I am always surprised. I may not remember having those thoughts, but they still exist and I know they are mine, and it's all part of making sense of who I am."
— Amy Tan

- Journals are an ideal way for some mourners to record thoughts and feelings.

- Remember—your inner thoughts and feelings of grief need to be expressed outwardly (which includes writing) if you are to heal.

- Consider jotting down your thoughts and feelings each night before you go to sleep. Your journal entries can be as long or as short as you want.

- One way to keep a grief journal is to write to the grandchild who died. Tell her about your day. Tell her how much you miss her. Tell her what you're struggling with most.

- Or keep a dream journal, instead. Keep a blank book on your nightstand for recording your dreams when you wake up.

- If you're not a writer, that's OK, too. Some people are journalers and some are not.

CARPE DIEM

Stop by your local bookstore and choose a blank book you like the look and feel of. Visit a coffee shop on your way home and write your first entry while enjoying your favorite beverage.

57.

ARRANGE FOR A FAMILY PHOTO

"You don't choose your family.
They are God's gift to you, as you are to them."
— Desmond Tutu

- Since your grandchild's death, you have probably become more aware of the importance of photos and family photos. You likely treasure special photos that capture your grandchild's smile and personality.

- Gather up all the photos you have of your grandchild, buy a collage frame, and spend an afternoon remembering and creating a photo collage to hang somewhere prominent.

- If you don't have any good photos of your grandchild to display in your home, ask another family member to help you track some down.

CARPE DIEM

Today, make plans for your next family photo. You could arrange
for an appointment at a photographer's studio, or you could simply
let all the family members know that at the next gathering, you've asked a
friend or neighbor to take a group photo with a high-resolution camera.
If you would like for the grandchild who died to be represented in the
photo, have someone in the group shot hold a large (maybe 8x10)
close-up photo of the missing child.

58.

PREPARE TO ANSWER "THE QUESTION"

"A grandparent's heart is a patchwork of love."
— Author unknown

- "How many grandchildren do you have?" What was once an everyday, friendly question is now a loaded gun.

- How will you answer? If you had three grandchildren and one dies, do you say you have two grandchildren? If you had a single grandchild and he dies, do you say you have no grandchildren? To many grieving grandparents, leaving out the child who died seems like disloyalty or, worse yet, like an erasure of the child's entire existence. Yet including the child who has died and then having to explain the death is a sure way to bog down an otherwise casual conversation.

- Most grieving grandparents come up with standard answers to "The Question," though their responses vary depending on whom they are talking to and in what situation. Here are a few of their ideas:

   - "I have two surviving grandkids. Mary is 10 and Alex is 3."
   - Simply: "Yes, I have grandchildren. Let me show you a picture. Mary is 10 and Alex is 3."
   - If you believe in an afterlife, you might say, "I have two grandchildren here on earth and one waiting for me in heaven."
   - If you had two grandchildren and one died: "I have two grandchildren. One is alive and one has died."
   - If your only grandchild died: "Yes, one grandson (or one granddaughter)." If the questions persist: "Jeff died when he as 16. That was three years ago."

- I'm told that answering "The Question" gets easier and more natural over time. You will discover how you are most comfortable responding to it.

CARPE DIEM
Talk with your spouse or a friend about how to handle "The Question" so you won't be caught so off-guard when the next person asks you.

59.

VISIT THE CEMETERY

"Ever since the Christmas of '53, I have felt that the yuletide is a special hell for those families who have suffered any loss; the so-called spirit of giving can be as greedy as receiving—Christmas is our time to be aware of what we lack, of who's not home."

— John Irving

- Visiting the cemetery or the place in which your grandchild's remains were scattered is an important mourning ritual for many grieving families. It helps them embrace their loss and remember the child who died.

- Some grieving grandparents spend time at the gravesite regularly. Some visit on holidays, birthdays, and anniversaries.

- Still others find no solace or meaning in visiting the cemetery. "That's not where my child is. He's in heaven!" one mother told me. If the cemetery isn't for you, that's fine, as long as you're not simply avoiding all reminders of your grandchild's death.

- Ask a friend or family member to go with you. You may feel comforted by their presence. Some grandparents have taught me that they prefer to go to the cemetery by themselves and that they find this a very spiritual time.

- Don't force others to visit the cemetery with you. Some grieving siblings have told me that they were forced to visit the cemetery and resented every minute of it. If your child and surviving grandchildren don't find visits to the cemetery healing, find other ways to mourn as a family.

CARPE DIEM

If you can, drop by the cemetery with a picnic lunch of foods that your grandchild loved best. Share the lunch with your spouse or a friend, or munch on it yourself while you think about your grandchild.

60.

START A NEW TRADITION

*"Create your own method. Don't depend slavishly on mine.
Make up something that will work for you!
But keep breaking traditions, I beg you."*
— Constantin Stanislavski

- Your family is grieving, but after the early, numb, shocked days and weeks of grief have passed, it may be time to consider how you will come together and still be a family without the presence of the child who died.

- For a fresh start, consider starting a new tradition. This is not an effort to forget the person who died, but rather a way for your family to reconsider their likes and dislikes, ingrained habits, and changing dynamics.

- Can you think of a fun group activity that your family has never tried as a group before? The age range and abilities of your gang will help you decide what might work. Bowling? Badminton? A pontoon boat outing?

- Starting a new tradition in honor of the child who died is another good idea. Many families create a fun annual event (which sometimes also doubles as a fundraiser) to remember the child as well as stay in touch with one another. Picnics, fun runs, and car washes are among the many possibilities.

CARPE DIEM
Spend a few minutes today with another family member
brainstorming ideas for a new family tradition.

61.

BREAK A BAD HABIT

"A change in bad habits leads to a change in life."
— Jenny Craig

- We all have bad habits. Some are minor transgressions (like leaving dirty socks on the floor), and some are more significant (like saying hurtful things when we are angry). I'd like you to pick a bad habit that hurts the people who love you. Keep in mind that some bad habits, like compromising our health by eating badly and/or being overweight, may not affect our families today—but they might in the near future if we were to get sick or die prematurely as a result of our behavior.

- Make a plan to break this habit. Talk to a friend or counselor about the habit and work, really work, to make a positive change.

- Do you have any bad habits that negatively affect, in particular, your grieving child (your grandchild's parent)? Maybe you don't call her as often as you should. Or maybe you have a tendency to make her feel bad about herself in some way. Now is the moment to rise to the occasion and make her feel as warmly and unconditionally loved and supported as possible.

- Imagine your grandchild looking down on you. For his sake, strive to be your best self, especially when it comes to your relationships with others.

CARPE DIEM

Make a list of your five most hurtful habits. Pick one. Ask someone else to help hold you accountable for working on breaking it.

62.

MEET YOUR GRANDCHILD IN "THIN PLACES"

"Sacred places are the truest definitions of the earth; they stand for the earth immediately and forever; they are its flags and shields. If you would know the earth for what it really is, learn it through its sacred places. You become one with a spirit that pervades geologic time and space."
— N. Scott Momaday

- In the Celtic tradition, "thin places" are spots where the separation between the physical world and the spiritual world seems tenuous. They are places where the veil between Heaven and earth, between the holy and the everyday, are so thin that when we are near them, we intuitively sense the timeless, boundless spiritual world.

- There is a Celtic saying that heaven and earth are only three feet apart, but in the thin places that distance is even smaller.

- Thin places are usually outdoors, often where water and land meet or land and sky come together. You might find thin places on a riverbank, a beach, or a mountaintop.

- Is there a thin place that is special to you, or better yet, that was special to both you and your grandchild? Go there to feed your spirit. See if you sense your grandchild's presence.

CARPE DIEM

Your thin places are anywhere that fills you with awe and a sense of wonder. They are spots that refresh your spirit and make you feel closer to God. Go to a thin place today and sit in contemplative silence.

63.

PLAN A CEREMONY

"Ritual is necessary for us to know anything."
— Ken Kesey

- A wise person once said: When words are inadequate, have a ceremony.

- Ceremony assists in reality, recall, support, expression, meaning, and transcendence.

- When personalized, the funeral ceremony can be a healing ritual. I hope the funeral for your precious grandchild was meaningful for you and your family. But ceremonies that take place later on can also be very meaningful.

- The ceremony might center on memories of your grandchild, "meaning of life" thoughts and feelings, or affirmation of faith.

CARPE DIEM
Hold a candle-lighting ceremony in memory of your grandchild. Invite a small group of friends and family who loved the child. Form a circle around a center candle, with each person holding their own small candle. Have each person light their candle from the center candle and share a memory. At the end, play a song or read a poem or prayer.

64.

MOVE BEYOND ANY BAD FEELINGS ABOUT THE FUNERAL

*"How could you go about choosing something that would
hold the half of your heart you had to bury?"*
— Jodi Picoult

- The death of a young person, especially a sudden death, often creates chaos in its wake. The family has to plan and carry out a funeral and burial arrangements at the very moment when they are most numb and in shock.

- Sometimes bad or hurtful funeral decisions get made in this situation. Some family members might feel snubbed. You might wish things had been done differently.

- Please know that everyone was doing the best they could at an impossible time. If hard feelings linger, try not to dwell on them but instead work to move past them.

- If you harbor bad feelings about the funeral or other decisions that were made at the time of the death, please share them with someone else outside the family. Talking about your feelings will help soften them. And if it's appropriate, gently communicate your grief over these decisions to your family—without placing blame. Try to make this conversation about everyone's struggle with grief, because that is the crossroads where you all meet and can help one another now.

CARPE DIEM
If you have any bad feelings about the funeral or decisions that were made
at the time of the death, share them with someone else today.

65.

CELEBRATE GRANDPARENT'S DAY

"Perfect love sometimes does not come until the first grandchild."
— Welsh proverb

- In the United States, Grandparent's Day is the first Sunday in September after Labor Day. It's not caught on nearly as well as Mother's Day and Father's Day, but that doesn't mean you can't celebrate it.

- If the holiday isn't a day that your children and grandchildren acknowledge by sending you cards and taking you out to dinner, that's OK. You can make the day a special day of connection between yourself and the child who died.

- Spend the day honoring and remembering your grandchild who died. Do something that reminds you of him or that you and he used to do together.

- You could also invite your surviving grandkids to spend the day with you. While you're together, take at least a few minutes to remember the child who died.

CARPE DIEM
Mark the next Grandparent's Day on your calendar and plan something in honor of your grandchild who died.

66.

MAKE YOUR GRANDCHILD'S FAVORITE MEAL

"Food is symbolic of love when words are inadequate."
— Alan D. Wolfelt

- When someone we love dies, they live on in us through memory. This is true—and important. But they can also live on in our families in ways that help us keep them close.

- What was your grandchild's favorite meal? Make it (or if it was a restaurant meal, go out to eat) and enjoy it with others who loved the person who died.

- There's something about sharing a meal that can open our hearts to sharing memories and kindnesses.

- Some people in your family might find it too painful to gather over the grandchild's favorite meal. That's OK. Not everyone has to participate this time. But if you continue to find ways to keep alive the child's memory, you can help create a family environment in which it's healthy to talk about death, share memories, and support one another.

CARPE DIEM
What was your grandchild's favorite dessert? Enjoy some today.

67.

TELL YOUR GRANDCHILDREN
YOUR LIFE STORIES

*"The one thing that you have that nobody else has is you.
Your voice, your mind, your story, your vision. So write and draw
and build and play and dance and live as only you can."*
— Neil Gaiman

- If you have surviving grandchildren, be sure to tell them all the stories you've been saving up your entire life.

- Your childhood was probably very different from theirs. Share what it was like to be kid-you, and show them photos to go with the stories.

- Kids also like to hear funny stories about what their own parents were like when they were kids.

- Ask your grandchildren to tell you stories from their lives too.

CARPE DIEM

Kids have short attention spans, and so for them, storytelling works best in small doses. Think up at least ten stories that you want to share with them. Make a written list so you don't forget! Then be sure to tell them one story each time you talk to them in the coming weeks.

68.

BREAK THE RULES

"Live one day at a time, emphasizing ethics rather than rules."
— Wayne Dyer

- One fantastic thing about growing older is that generally speaking, younger people start to give us some extra leeway.

- Allow yourself the same latitude. Grocery shopping in slippers? Sure thing! Ignoring the daily news? Oh well. Dessert for dinner? Why not?

- When it comes to grief and mourning, there aren't many rules…except the needs of mourning I listed near the beginning of this book (Ideas 10-15). And as long as you're reaching out to others and opening your heart, anything goes.

- You might have been taught certain grief etiquette, and yes, much of it is actually helpful, to yourself and others. Practices such as sending flowers really are meaningful. But you don't have to follow all the rules, especially if you see an opportunity to connect in a better way. For example, instead of writing a thank you note to a friend who made a donation in your grandchild's memory, how about taking that person out to lunch and sharing your thoughts and feelings about the child's death?

CARPE DIEM
As long as it won't hurt anyone, break a rule today.
Choose something that will make you or a loved one happy.

69.

SAY WHAT YOU NEED TO SAY

"When we were children, we used to think that when we were grown-up we would no longer be vulnerable. But to grow up is to accept vulnerability… To be alive is to be vulnerable."
— Madeleine L'Engle

- The death of your grandchild may have you thinking about things you wish you had said but never did. These kinds of regrets are normal, and none of us says or does everything that perhaps we should. It's just part of being human.

- But now you may realize that you have an opportunity to say things to those who are still alive.

- Don't wait! None of us ever knows for sure how much precious time on Earth we have left. Don't let another day go by without telling those you love how much they mean to you.

CARPE DIEM

Make a special, individual lunch or dinner date with the most special people in your life—one person at a time. Just the two of you will celebrate your relationship, catch up, and spend an hour or two basking in your love for one another. Over dessert (and yes, there really should be at least a bite or two of dessert for this dinner), take this person's hands in yours and tell him how you feel about him.

70.

BE MINDFUL OF ANNIVERSARIES

"That was the thing. You never got used to it, the idea of someone being gone. Just when you think it's reconciled, accepted, someone points it out to you, and it just hits you all over again, that shocking."
— Sarah Dessen

- Anniversaries—of the death, life events, birthdays—are typically difficult for grieving families. Days that used to be so very special are now painful reminders of what has been lost.

- These are times you may want to plan ahead for. Perhaps you could take the lead in planning a tree-planting ceremony on the anniversary of the death. Maybe on your grandchild's next birthday you could visit the cemetery or host a small family gathering.

- For some grieving parents and grandparents, the anticipation of the anniversary or the days immediately following the anniversary are more difficult than the anniversary day itself. Be in touch with your child as the date approaches and offer ideas about how you could spend the day together.

- Don't expect your friends to remember these important days. Instead, be proactive and reach out to them. Make plans. Talk about your feelings with a close friend.

CARPE DIEM
What's the next anniversary you've been dreading? Make a plan right now for what you will do on that day. Reach out to your grieving child about her plans and offer your support.

71.

VISIT THE GREAT OUTDOORS

*"The human spirit needs places where nature has not been
rearranged by the hand of man."*
— Author unknown

- For many people, it is restorative and energizing to spend time outside.

- Mourners often find nature's timeless beauty healing. The sound of a bird singing or the awesome presence of a lake or a river can help put things in perspective.

- Go on a nature walk. Or camping. Or canoeing. The farther away from civilization, the better.

- Where did your grandchild like to be outdoors? Have you visited this place recently? If not, make a point to spend some time there in the near future.

- Experience the elements. Take time to feel the rain, wind, or snow.

CARPE DIEM
Call your local parks department or area forest service
(or look online) for a map of nearby walking or hiking trails.
Take a nature walk sometime this week.

72.

WATCH FOR WARNING SIGNS

*"When you are compassionate with yourself, you trust in your soul,
which you let guide your life. Your soul knows the geography
of your destiny better than you do."*
— John O'Donohue

- Understandably, sometimes grieving parents and grandparents fall back on self-destructive behaviors to get through this difficult time.

- Try to be honest with yourself about drug or alcohol abuse. If you're in over your head, ask someone for help. If others approach you about your substance abuse, let them in.

- Of course, mental illness and personality problems that were present before the death can also complicate grief.

- Seeing a grief counselor is probably a good idea for parents or grandparents who are also struggling with substance abuse, clinical depression, or other mental health-related problem. You may simply not be able to reconcile your grief and continue your life in a meaningful way without professional help.

- Are you seriously considering suicide? Put this book down right now and talk to someone about your depression.

- If you are seeing red-flag behaviors not in yourself but in your grieving child, don't hesitate to talk to her about it as well as marshal the intervention of others. As the person who may know her best, you just might be the one to save her.

CARPE DIEM
Acknowledging to ourselves that we have a problem may come too late.
If someone suggests that you need help, consider yourself
lucky to be so well loved and get help.

73.

UPDATE YOUR WILL

*"You have not lived today until you have done something
for someone who can never repay you."*
— John Bunyan

- The grandchild who died may have been named in your will. Now that she is gone, you may want to update your will to reflect this new reality.

- But wait! I'm not suggesting that you necessarily "write her out" of your will. Instead, I'd like you to consider honoring her memory in your will.

- What did she love? What causes did she support? While you can't leave this grandchild money or property, you can specify that some or all of the money and property that would have gone to her will now joyfully be given to a charity or cause she was passionate about.

- Think about her school, her hobbies, her teams, and her loves.

- If your grandchild was older and had a partner and/or children, you may also choose to apportion a share of your money and property to them in her stead. Wouldn't she love that idea?

CARPE DIEM
Make an appointment with your attorney to have your will updated.
If you don't yet have a will, now's a good time to make one!

74.

MOVE

"It's helpful to realize that this very body that we have, that's sitting right here right now…with its aches and its pleasures…is exactly what we need to be fully human, fully awake, fully alive."

— Pema Chodron

- We all know how important physical activity is to our physical health, but did you know that it also has a significant effect on your mood? Research shows that exercise helps lift anxiety and ease depression.

- In the early days and weeks of your grief, you will likely feel tired. Honor your body's natural "lethargy of grief" by laying your body down three times a day for at least 20 minutes. But later on, forcing yourself to get moving every day will help you feel better.

- I often tell mourners that they need to put their grief into motion by expressing it. This movement of thoughts and feelings is what creates opportunity for positive change. Similarly, moving your body creates physical and biochemical change that supports the healing of grief.

- Social activity combined with physical activity is a great double whammy. Walk regularly with a friend or play golf with your buddies and you're benefitting physically, emotionally, socially, and, I would argue, spiritually!

CARPE DIEM

Get at least half an hour of physical activity today—more if your fitness level is high. You don't need to go to a gym! Gardening, housework, and all kinds of everyday activities count.

75.

LISTEN TO THE MUSIC

"Music expresses feeling and thought, without language; it was below and before speech, and it is above and beyond all words."
— Robert G. Ingersoll

- Music can be very healing to mourners because it helps us access our feelings, both happy and sad. Music can soothe the spirit and nurture the heart.

- All types of music can be healing—rock & roll, classical, blues, folk.

- Consider listening to music you normally don't, perhaps the opera or the symphony. Or make a recording of your favorite songs, all together on one tape.

- Do you play an instrument or sing? Allow yourself the time to try these activities again soon.

- What kind of music did your grandchild love? Have you listened to it lately? Ask for a list of her favorites and spend a rainy afternoon really listening to the music.

- Because music is the language of the soul, it can also be painful at times. If music brings comfort, then listen. If not, don't.

CARPE DIEM
Visit a music store today (or go online) and sample a few CDs or tracks.
Buy yourself the one that moves you the most.

76.

LAUGH

*"Every parent who loses a child finds a way to laugh again.
The timbre begins to fade. The edge dulls. The hurt lessens.
Every love is carved from loss. Mine was. Yours is. Your great-great-
great-grandchildren's will be. But we learn to live in that love."*

— Jonathan Safran Foer

- Humor is one of the most healing gifts of humanity.

- Laughter restores hope and assists us in surviving the pain of grief. If you're of faith, perhaps you'll relate to Proverbs 15:13: "A merry heart is good medicine for the soul."

- It's OK to laugh even though your grandchild has died. You can laugh and enjoy things even as you miss your grandchild very much. In fact, laughing is a way of honoring the child's spirit.

- What made your grandchild laugh? Silly jokes? Slapstick comedy? Intellectual humor? Enjoy some of his brand of humor today.

CARPE DIEM

Try to remember one time in particular that your grandchild laughed and laughed. Close your eyes and immerse yourself in this moment. See if you can recall your grandchild's face and the sound of his laughter.

77.

CRY

"Sometimes allowing yourself to cry is the scariest thing you'll ever do. And the bravest. It takes a lot of courage to face the facts, stare loss in the face, bare your heart, and let it bleed. But it is the only way to cleanse your wounds and prepare them for healing."

— Barbara Johnson

- Tears are a natural cleansing and healing mechanism. It's OK to cry. In fact, it's good to cry when you feel like it. What's more, tears are a form of mourning. They are sacred!

- On the other hand, don't feel bad if you aren't crying a lot. Not everyone is a crier. Some men, in particular, do not feel the need to cry, especially as the death grows more distant. The inability to cry is not necessarily a deficit.

- You may find that those around you are uncomfortable with your tears. As a society, we're often not so good at witnessing others in pain.

- Explain to your friends and family that you need to cry right now and that they can help by allowing you to.

- You may find yourself crying at unexpected times or places. If you need to, excuse yourself and retreat to somewhere private.

CARPE DIEM

If you feel like it, have a good cry today. Find a safe place to embrace your pain, and cry as long and as hard as you want to.

78.

PRAY

"Prayer is a path where there is none."
— Noah Benshea

- Prayer often comes naturally for grieving grandparents. At night when you go to bed and in the morning when you wake up, where else is there to turn for the kind of help you need? If you feel unable to pray, you might ask others to pray on your behalf.

- Besides, studies have shown that prayer can actually help people heal.

- If you believe in a higher power, pray. Pray for your grandchild. Pray for your child. Pray for your questions about life and death to be answered. Pray for the strength to embrace your pain and to heal over time. Pray for others affected by this death.

- Many places of worship have prayer lists. Call your place of worship and ask that your name be added to the prayer list. On worship day, the whole congregation will pray for you. Often many individuals will pray at home for those on the prayer list, as well.

- Some faiths have ongoing prayers that are said for the dead. Mourning Jews (traditionally males) say a special daily prayer called the Kaddish. Perhaps creating a daily prayer ritual—designating a time, place, and prayer to pray each day—would provide a systematic and healing outlet for your grief.

CARPE DIEM
Bow your head right now and say a silent prayer. If you are out of practice, don't worry; just let your thoughts flow naturally.

79.

AVOID SAYING "SHOULD"

"Advice is like castor oil—easy enough to give, but dreadful uneasy to take."
— Josh Billings

- Each person's grief is unique. Your grief since your grandchild's death is different from your child's grief. Your child's grief is different from her spouse's grief. What's more, there's no one right way or timetable to express the grief.

- Keep the uniqueness of grief in mind as you try to help your grieving child. Parenting adult children is always challenging (because none of us is ever done being a parent!), but it's especially hard after the death of one of your child's children. As you try to help, avoid telling your child what she "should" be doing or what she "should not" be feeling. First of all, she's the expert of her own grief. And second, phrasing your suggestions in this way can sound judgmental at a time when she needs unconditional acceptance.

- Instead of saying, "You should get some sleep," try, "I'll watch Joey tonight. Maybe you can get some sleep." Instead of saying, "You shouldn't feel guilty," try, "It hurts my heart that you blame yourself. You are such a loving mother."

- "You need to…" and "You have to…" are other sentence-starters to watch out for.

CARPE DIEM
The next time you catch yourself saying "should" to your grieving child, stop…and try to rephrase. Own your own thoughts, feelings, and actions, but try not to tell her what hers "should" be.

80.

STEADY THE KEEL

"Most of life is showing up. You do the best you can, which varies from day to day."
— Regina Brett

- When an entire family is reeling in the aftermath of the death of a young person, there is no predicting how each day will unfold.

- Family members will react differently from each other. On any given day, they may also react differently than they themselves did just a few days earlier. Your own grief will ebb and flow and change as time passes.

- No matter how hard you are trying to mourn in healthy ways yourself, as well as support your grieving child and family, the weeks and months to come will be challenging. In addition to experiencing the normal and necessary pain of loss, family members will likely hurt each other's feelings on occasion. Disagreements will arise. All the hurts together may seem unsurvivable on some days.

- Yet as the member of your family with significant life experience, you can help steady the keel. You know that petty arguments and criticisms borne of the natural stress after a death will indeed happen…yet they need not do lasting damage to important relationships.

- Take things one day at a time. Encourage others in your family to do the same. Every day is a new day. Keep showing up.

CARPE DIEM

The next time a bad grief day hurts feelings in your family, arrange for a family get-together and help everyone be their best selves.

81.

WRITE A THANK-YOU NOTE

"If the only prayer you said was thank you, that would be enough."
— Meister Eckhart

- Recognizing and expressing gratitude opens our hearts and strengthens our relationships. It's a big part of what helps us live and love fully until we die.

- Write one thank you note every day until you can't think of one more person to thank.

- Take the long view, and look back on your entire life. I'll bet there are many, many people who touched your life in some small but important way. How many of them have you thanked?

- What about your closest friends and family? Have you sat down with each of them, one-on-one, to express your love and gratitude?

- Don't forget the people who make your everyday life more pleasant— your mail carrier, your neighbor, your doctor, your vet, etc.

CARPE DIEM

Today, write a thank you note to someone who cared for or was special to your grandchild. Tell this person how much you miss your grandchild but how grateful you are that he helped fill your grandchild's days on Earth with love and laughter.

82.

WRITE A LETTER TO YOUR GRANDCHILD

"A grandchild fills a space in your heart that you never knew was empty."
— Author unknown

- Some of us talk openly and out loud to our loved ones who pass on before we do. But others among us are a bit shyer about sharing our internal thoughts and feelings.

- If you wish you could talk to your grandchild one more time, write him a letter. Tell him everything you wish you had said but didn't. Tell him whatever is on your mind and in your heart.

- What do you remember most from when you were his age? How was his life different than yours? Tell him your most precious stories.

- What will you do with this letter once you've finished writing it? Consider giving it to your grandchild's parents or siblings. Leaving it at his grave is another possibility. Or, maybe you would rather tuck it into a drawer and reread it every year on the anniversary of the death. (If you're like me, you'll also need to make yourself a reminder about where you've hidden it!)

CARPE DIEM
Buy a beautiful card or piece of stationery today and write a
long, old-fashioned letter to your grandchild.

83.

WRITE LETTERS TO BE READ
ON A FUTURE DATE

"How wonderful it is to be able to write someone a letter! To feel like conveying your thoughts to a person, to sit at your desk and pick up a pen, to put your thoughts into words like this is truly marvelous."

— Haruki Murakami

- One of the joys of being an older person is that younger people often respect your experience and believe that you have wisdom to share.

- Whether we can call it wisdom or not, we certainly have perspective on and hard-won understanding of many important things in life.

- If you have young grandchildren still on this Earth with you, you may want to share some of your life story and wisdom with them when they get older. Consider writing it down today.

- You can also write letters to your child or other special people to be opened upon your death.

CARPE DIEM

Buy some nice stationery and write a letter today to be opened either upon your death or on a certain, specified date, such as your grandson's 18th birthday. Give the letter to your attorney or someone who will safeguard it for you yet not forget it exists.

84.

REMEMBER OTHERS WHO HAD A SPECIAL RELATIONSHIP WITH YOUR GRANDCHILD

"Funny thing how when you reach out, people tend to reach right back. Best, then, to make sure your hand is open and not fisted."
— Richelle E. Goodrich

- At times your appropriately inward focus will make you feel alone in your grief. Grieving parents and grandparents, especially, are often so immersed in their own grief in the early weeks and months after the death that they cannot empathize with others who loved the child.

- Yet maybe you're now ready to think about others who were affected by the death of your grandchild: friends, boyfriends or girlfriends, teachers, neighbors, coworkers.

- Is there someone outside of the inner "circle of mourners" who may be struggling with this death? Perhaps you could write her a note of support and thanks for the love and friendship she gave to your grandchild.

- Grieving children, especially, need our love and support. If your grandchild was young when she died, her friends need opportunities to mourn. Maybe you could invite them to your house or take them shopping for an afternoon. With their parents' permission, talk to them about the death and their thoughts and feelings.

CARPE DIEM
Today, write and mail a brief supportive note to someone else affected by the death.

85.

DON'T BE ALARMED BY "GRIEFBURSTS"

"In the first few months of my grief, nothing could distract me from the sorrow and pain. When you quit trying to avoid the breakdowns, the grief bursts, the weeping episodes, you feel better. I don't think you can force yourself to stop. People try, but it's ultimately what keeps them from healing."

— J.S. Jacobs

- Sometimes heightened periods of sadness overwhelm grieving grandparents. These moments can seem to come of out nowhere and can be frightening and painful.

- Even long after the death, something as simple as a sound, a smell, or a phrase can bring on a "griefburst." You might hear a name, see a toy, or touch a fabric that suddenly reminds you of your grandchild and all your family has lost.

- Allow yourself to experience griefbursts without shame or self-judgment, no matter where and when they occur. (Sooner or later, one will probably happen when you're surrounded by people, maybe even strangers.) If you would feel more comfortable, retreat to somewhere private when these strong feelings surface.

- Don't isolate yourself in an attempt to protect yourself from griefbursts, however. Staying cooped up at home all the time is not self-compassion: it's self-destruction.

CARPE DIEM

Create an action plan for your next griefburst. For example, you might plan to drop whatever you are doing and go for a walk or record thoughts in your journal.

86.

MEND FENCES

"But grief makes a monster out of us sometimes…and sometimes you say and do things to the people you love that you can't forgive yourself for."
— Melina Marchetta

- If old hurts or transgressions are hindering any significant relationships in your life, now may be the time to mend fences.

- One of the six needs of mourning is receiving (and accepting) help from others. A number of your family members probably need support right now, but if "bad blood" is separating some of you, how can you help each other?

- We can't change other people, but we can change our own behavior. And sometimes when we say "I'm sorry" (even if what happened wasn't clearly our fault), we open a closed door just enough to let love flow through again.

- Yes, sometimes it's better to set boundaries so that toxic people can't enter at all. But often, we can rebuild relationships with even "difficult" people by simply offering an olive branch and approaching with kindness.

- Your child needs as much love and support as possible right now. So do you. So does everyone else affected by this death. Peacemaking can help light the path on the journey to healing.

CARPE DIEM

What one relationship in your life is the most strained? Is it a source of pain for you? If so, the pain is a sign that you should express your thoughts and feelings. Find someone else who's a good listener and unburden yourself today. Consider next steps.

87.

GET A NEW PERSPECTIVE

"What we see depends mainly on what we look for."
— John Lubbock

- The older we get, the easier it is to get stuck in familiar, and therefore comfortable, routines.

- When we're grieving, we often lack the energy to do anything more than we have to. In the early weeks and months of grief, our simple routines help us survive.

- But later on, as our grief journey continues, we may start to feel stuck. Despair and joylessness can become entrenched. If this happens to you, it might be time to shake things up a bit.

- As with trying something new, going to new places can give us new perspective. Do you always go to the same grocery store? Try a different one. Do you walk the same route every day? Walk somewhere else. Do you always attend the same church service or drive the same routes? Diversify!

- Taking a vacation, somewhere away from your day-to-day life, can also help. You'll find that your grief accompanies you, but the mere fact of looking at it from a new vantage point may help you befriend and soften it.

CARPE DIEM

Go somewhere you've never been today, preferably somewhere out of character for you. It could be something as simple as trying a new ethnic restaurant or visiting a museum you've never been to in your own town.

88.

START, RENEW, OR GIVE AWAY A COLLECTION

*"I believe that everyone collects.
I think collecting is in our blood as humans."*
— Lynda Resnick

- When someone we love dies, we often feel despair at the lack of control. We would have prevented this death if we could have. But we couldn't.

- In many ways, life is out of our control. This is a painful lesson that those of us of enhanced age have learned many times.

- But we do have control over some things! Importantly, we can control how we live and how we love. Collections are essentially a form of taking control and keeping order.

- Throughout your life, you may have collected a number of different things. With collecting, the thrill of the hunt is half the fun. If you still enjoy collecting, spend some time doing it this week. If you're done collecting, maybe you have a collection you could pass along to someone who would enjoy it.

- Consider starting a new collection (or enhancing an old one) that reminds you of your grandchild. If she loved owls, you could collect owl memorabilia. If she loved the beach, you could start a shell collection. Each moment you spend seeking out a new piece for your collection is a moment you will spend honoring her memory and communing with her spirit.

CARPE DIEM
Today, start, renew, or give away a collection. Or if collecting doesn't interest you personally but you know a collector, spend some time with him today learning about his collection.

89.

PRACTICE RANDOM ACTS OF KINDNESS AND SENSELESS ACTS OF BEAUTY

"You will lose someone you can't live without, and your heart will be badly broken, and the bad news is that you never completely get over the loss of your beloved. But this is also the good news. They live forever in your broken heart that doesn't seal back up. And you come through. It's like having a broken leg that never heals perfectly—that still hurts when the weather gets cold, but you learn to dance with the limp."

— Anne Lamott

- If this Idea sounds familiar to you, it's because it's a bumper sticker. Have you seen it?

- After you emerge from the early weeks and months of your grief, you may find that you once again have the energy to really live. Or perhaps this death has awakened in you the realization that today is indeed the first day of the rest of your life.

- Your family has been wounded, leaving a gaping, gasping hole. Nobody can fill the hole created by the loss of your grandchild. But kindness, love, and beauty can make life worth living again.

- Every day, be kind to someone else for no good reason. When you notice or make something beautiful, share it with someone else.

CARPE DIEM

Extend an out-of-the-ordinary kindness to your grieving child today, such as giving her flowers or making her favorite dessert.

90.

REDEFINE WHAT BEING A GRANDPARENT MEANS TO YOU

"It's amazing how grandparents seem so young once you become one."
— Author unknown

- In the Introduction, I talked a little about what the word "grandparent" literally means. Culturally, we have also created clichés and formed expectations about what grandparents do and don't do.

- Here are some common stereotypes: Grandparents are stodgy. They're conservative with their money. They talk about their aches and pains. They eat dinner early and go to bed early. They have gray, short hair. They don't understand the younger generation.

- You may or may not embody some of these characteristics, and none of them is wrong or bad. But here's the thing: You can be whatever sort of grandparent you want to be. Physical limitations of aging aside (and boy am I ever beginning to understand those!), you get to define how to live out your "golden years."

- If you have other grandchildren, your relationship with them is largely in your control. If you would like to be closer to them, then get closer. Break free of whatever preconceptions may be holding you back and just go for it. If you don't have remaining grandchildren, you may be able to express that grandparently love in other ways, by volunteering, for example, or getting involved in your neighborhood.

CARPE DIEM

Today, think about your own grandparents. How were they different from you? How were they similar? Share these memories with someone else.

91.

TAKE THINGS ONE DAY AT A TIME

"Life is like an ice-cream cone. You have to lick it one day at a time."
— Charles M. Schulz

- Your grief will feel different on different days. Some days will naturally be harder than others.

- Yet each day is a new opportunity—to grieve and mourn, yes, but also to love and to connect.

- When I have a particularly rough day, I sometimes picture a chalkboard covered with all the emotions and conversations and happenings of that day. Then in my imagination, as I lie in bed with my eyes closed, I erase the messy chalkboard. When I'm done erasing, I have a "clean slate" to start with the next morning.

- Take things one day at a time. That's all there is.

CARPE DIEM
Start each new day with a meditation or prayer that helps you live from the heart and be open to all the blessings of that day.

92.

TAKE A CHANCE

*"Parting is inevitably painful. It's like an amputation,
I feel a limb is being torn off, without which I shall be unable to
function. And yet, once it is done… life rushes back into the void,
richer, more vivid and fuller than before."*
— Anne Morrow Lindbergh

- If you're a grandparent, no matter how old you are, you've lived long enough to have earned yourself some latitude.

- Go ahead—let your hair down. Get fearless. What do you have to lose?

- I'm not talking about taking stupid chances or doing things that take you out of reality (like drugs). I'm talking about things that immerse you more boldly into reality and affirm life.

- What have you always wanted to do but have never had the courage to try? Open mic night at the local stand-up comedy joint? Dying your hair auburn? Line dancing? Skydiving? Traveling to an exotic locale?

- Your grief may be making you feel that life is no longer worth living. Pick an activity that helps relight your divine spark and refreshes your outlook on life.

CARPE DIEM
Today, schedule an activity you've always wanted to try
but have been a little (or a lot!) afraid of.

93.

IMAGINE THE GRANDCHILD WHO DIED IN HEAVEN

"Never. We never lose our loved ones. They accompany us; they don't disappear from our lives. We are merely in different rooms."
— Paulo Coelho

- Do you believe in an afterlife? Many mourners I have had the honor of companioning in their journeys are comforted by a belief or a hope that somehow, somewhere, their loved one lives on in health and happiness. For some, this belief is anchored in a religious faith. For others, it is simply a spiritual sense.

- If you do believe in an afterlife, you probably take comfort in having a continued spiritual relationship with the grandchild who died. You may even have open, loving conversations with her.

- You may also find solace in knowing that your grandchild was welcomed and is being cared for by other family members and dear friends who died before he did.

CARPE DIEM

Close your eyes right now and imagine what heaven might be like. See your grandchild strong and smiling. Imagine her waving to you. And imagine your reunion with her when, one day, you come to join her.

94.

ESTABLISH A MEMORIAL FUND OR SCHOLARSHIP IN THE NAME OF YOUR GRANDCHILD

"We make a living by what we get. We make a life by what we give."
— Winston Churchill

- Sometimes bereaved families ask that memorial contributions be made to specified charities in the name of the child who died. This practice allows friends and family members to show their support while helping the family feel that something good came of the death.

- You can establish a personalized and ongoing memorial to your grandchild, even if you're not wealthy. Some families organize yearly yard sales. Some establish scholarship funds. Some donate each year to a certain charity. Some establish school awards in the child's name. Consider being the one to present the award or scholarship to the recipients.

- What was meaningful to your grandchild? Did she love a sport or a hobby? Did she have empathy for a certain group of people? Was she affected by a certain illness?

- Your local bank or funeral home may have ideas about how to go about setting up a memorial fund.

CARPE DIEM
Call a friend or talk to your family and together brainstorm a list of ideas for a memorial. Then take it one step further and make a phone call for additional information.

95.

REASSESS YOUR PRIORITIES

"The life you have left is a gift. Cherish it. Enjoy it now, to the fullest.
Do what matters, now."

— Leo Babauta

• Death has a way of making us rethink our lives and the meaningfulness of the ways we spend them. The death of a young person, in particular, tends to awaken grieving parents and grandparents to what is truly meaningful in life.

• What gives your life meaning? What doesn't? Take steps to spend more of your time on the former and less on the latter.

• Now may be the time to reconfigure your life. Choose a satisfying new second career or hobby. Go back to school. Begin volunteering. Help others in regular, ongoing ways. Move closer to your children and surviving grandchildren.

• Many mourners have told me that they can no longer stand to be around people who seem shallow, egocentric, or mean-spirited. It's OK to let friendships wither with friends whom these adjectives now seem to describe. Instead, find ways to connect with people who share your new outlook on life—and death.

CARPE DIEM:

Make a list with two columns: What's important to me.
What's not. Brainstorm for at least 15 minutes.

96.

LEAVE A LEGACY

"It is never too late to be who you might have been."
— George Eliot

- The older we get, the more we tend to look back on our lives and wonder what all our days have amounted to.

- What are you most proud of? What are the good things people will say about you at your funeral? Never pass up an opportunity to celebrate and have gratitude for your accomplishments and the meaningful connections you've had with others.

- What are not so proud of? What have been your shortcomings? None of us is perfect (I'm certainly not!), so I'm not asking you to shame yourself for bad choices or wasted opportunities. Instead, I'm asking you to remember that you are still alive. It is not too late to apologize, make amends, or change your behavior.

- What will your legacies be? You might have different legacies in your work life, your community life, and your family life. Now that you've achieved some wisdom, which legacies feel most important to you, and how can you spend your remaining days striving to be your best self?

CARPE DIEM
Write your own obituary today, the way you would like it to read.
Then get out there and live up to it.

97.

LIVE FOR YOUR GRANDCHILD

"Grief is forever. It doesn't go away; it becomes a part of you, step for step, breath for breath. I will never stop grieving Bailey because I will never stop loving her. That's just how it is. Grief and love are conjoined; you don't get one without the other. All I can do is love her, and love the world, emulate her by living with daring and spirit and joy."

— Jandy Nelson

- Your grandchild's life was cut short. That is so unfair, and I am sorry. As many grieving grandparents do, you may wish it was you who had died instead. You may wish you could trade places.

- But you didn't die. You are still here. If you choose to, you can take this reality as a sign that you still have work to do and gifts to share here on Earth.

- Choose to live. Choose to be your best self. Choose to share your unique talents. Choose to love and connect.

- Your grandchild was cheated out of decades of life. Don't make his death even more of a waste by frittering away your precious remaining years. Instead, live for your grandchild. Make him proud of how you spend each and every day.

CARPE DIEM
Do something today that your grandchild would be delighted about.

98.

UNDERSTAND THE CONCEPT OF "RECONCILIATION"

"And you do come out of it, that's true. After a year, after five.
But you don't come out of it like a train coming out of a tunnel, bursting
through the downs into sunshine...; you come out of it as a gull comes out
of an oil-slick. You are tarred and feathered for life."

— Julian Barnes

- Sometimes you'll hear about mourners "recovering" from or "getting over" grief. These terms are damaging because it implies that grief is an illness that must be cured. It also connotes an eventual return to the way things were before the death.

- As you know, becoming a grandparent is a permanent change in a man or woman's life. Just as grandparents don't get over being grandparents, they don't get over their grief. Instead, they become "reconciled" to it. In other words, they learn to live with it and are forever changed by it.

- This does not mean a life of misery, however. Mourners often not only heal but grow through grief. Our lives can potentially be deeper and more meaningful after the death of someone we love.

- In reconciliation, the sharp pangs of grief soften and painful thoughts and feelings subside. A renewed enjoyment of today and interest in the future begins to overtake that natural obsession with the past. Days are happier than sad. New goals are set and worked toward. Bonds with other people are strengthened and enjoyed. Hope is refreshed.

CARPE DIEM
Have you begun to reconcile your grief?
If so, what does reconciliation feel like for you?

99.

LIVE EACH DAY LIKE IT'S YOUR LAST

"Only people who are capable of loving strongly can also suffer great sorrow, but this same necessity of loving serves to counteract their grief and heals them."
— Leo Tolstoy

- Your precious grandchild's life here on Earth was cut short. Yet you live on.

- Don't you think you owe it to your grandchild to live fully? Don't you think you owe it to yourself to live fully?

- Imagine your grandchild looking down on you from heaven. Is she happy with how you're spending your days?

- What if today were your last? What if you knew that when you went to bed tonight, you would never wake up? How would you spend today? Do that.

CARPE DIEM

Today, make a list of 10 things you would definitely do if today were your last day. Do one of them each day for the next 10 days.

100.

EMBRACE THE WAYS IN WHICH YOU ARE GROWING THROUGH GRIEF

"You gain strength by every experience in which you really stop to look fear in the face. You must do the thing you think you cannot do."

— Eleanor Roosevelt

- You may find that you are growing emotionally and spiritually as a result of your grief journey. I understand that you've paid the ultimate price for this growth and that you would gladly trade it for one more minute with your grandchild. Still, the death may have brought bittersweet gifts into your life that you would not otherwise have.

- Many grieving families emerge from the early years of grief as stronger, more capable people. They're more assertive and apt to say what they really believe and be who they are. They don't put up with baloney. They've already survived the worst life has to offer, so anything still to come can't be so bad. And they've learned what's truly important and what's not.

- What's more, many grieving grandparents discover depths of compassion for others that they never knew they had. Lots volunteer, many undertake daily kindnesses, virtually all are more emotionally and spiritually tuned-in to others and more interpersonally effective.

CARPE DIEM
Consider the ways in which you may be "growing through grief."

A FINAL WORD

"One of the most powerful handclasps is that of a new grandbaby around the finger of a grandparent."
— Joy Hargrove

Most of us who are privileged to have lived beyond the half-century mark are also all too aware of the bittersweet possibilities that are part and parcel of living so long. Chief among them is the increasingly likely possibility that we will outlive at least some of the people we love best.

Not our children, we hope—and certainly not their children. But all too often, despite our fervent prayers, such an abominable death comes to pass. No one should have to bury a grandchild.

Yet here you are. I am so sorry for your loss. And here I am, reaching out to you across the page. I hope that you have found a measure of affirmation, guidance, and consolation in this little book.

My prayer for you

May you find the courage to mourn well so that you can live and love well, every single one of your remaining days.

May you honestly express all of your thoughts and feelings about your grandchild's death, and never stop expressing them.

May you support your grieving child and family—and also reach out for support for yourself.

May you rise each day with the intention to remember and honor your grandchild.

May you strive to be your best, most authentic self, the person that your grandchild loves and would be most proud of.

Right now, take a moment to close your eyes, open your heart, and remember the one-of-a-kind smile of your precious grandchild.

Bless you. I hope we meet one day.

THE GRIEVING
GRANDPARENT'S CODE:

Ten Inalienable Rights
As You Journey Through Grief

Though you should reach out to others as you journey through grief after
the death of your grandchild, you should not feel obligated to accept the
unhelpful responses you may receive from some people. You are the one who
is grieving, and as such, you have certain "rights" no one should try to take
away from you.

The following list is intended both to empower you to heal and to decide how
others can and cannot help. This is not to discourage you from reaching out
to others for help, but rather to assist you in distinguishing useful responses
from hurtful ones.

1. **You have the right to experience your own unique grief.** No one else will
   grieve the death of your grandchild exactly as you do. So, when you turn to
   others for help, don't allow them to tell what you should or should not be
   feeling.

2. **You have the right to get support for yourself as you support your
   family.** Often, grieving grandparents must put the needs of their grieving
   child and family before their own. If this happens to you, be sure to get
   support for yourself from others outside the family.

3. **You have the right to feel a multitude of emotions.** Shock, helplessness,
   fear, guilt, and relief are just a few of the emotions you might feel after the
   death of a grandchild. Feelings are not right or wrong—they just are. Find
   listeners who will accept your feelings without condition.

4. **You have the right to be tolerant of your physical and emotional limits.**
   As you're mourning your grandchild's death, your grief will probably leave

you feeling fatigued. Respect what your body and mind are telling you. Get daily rest. Eat balanced meals. And don't allow others to push you into doing things you don't feel ready to do.

5. **You have the right to experience "griefbursts."** Sometimes, out of nowhere, a powerful surge of grief may overcome you—even long after your grandchild's death. This can be frightening, but it is normal and natural. Find someone who understands and will let you talk it out.

6. **You have the right to make use of ritual.** After the death of your grandchild, the funeral and other ceremonies are essential in helping you with reality, recall, support, expression, meaning, and transcendence. Remember, when words are inadequate, turn to ritual.

7. **You have the right to embrace your spirituality.** The grief you experience after the death of a grandchild is, in essence, a spiritual journey. Seek the company of people who understand and support your unique and possibly changing spirituality.

8. **You have the right to search for meaning.** This death was untimely and out of order. You may find yourself asking, "Why did he die? Why this way? Why now?" Some of your questions may have answers, but some may not. Trust in the journey.

9. **You have the right to treasure your memories.** Memories are one of the best legacies that exist after the death of someone you love. You will always remember your precious grandchild. Instead of setting your memories aside, find ways to share them.

10. **You have the right to move toward your grief and heal.** Reconciling your grief over the loss of your grandchild will not happen quickly. Remember, grief is best experienced in "doses." Be patient and tolerant with yourself and avoid people who are impatient and intolerant with you. Neither you nor those around you must forget that the death of a grandchild changes your life forever.

ALSO BY ALAN WOLFELT

Healing a Parent's Grieving Heart
100 Practical Ideas After Your Child Dies

The unthinkable has happened: your child has died. The normal circle of life has been broken and you have outlived your child. How do you go on? What can you do with your pain? Where do you turn? What do other grieving parents do not only to survive, but over time and with the support of others, to live and love fully again?

This book offers 100 practical ideas that have helped other grieving parents understand and reconcile their grief. Common challenges for grieving parents, such as dealing with marital stress, helping surviving siblings, dealing with hurtful advice, and exploring feelings of guilt, are also addressed. Whether your child was young or an adult, whether your loss was recent or many years ago, this compassionate and easy-to-use resource will be a source of comfort and healing.

"Access to this kind of help when my daughter died would have made a major difference in my grief. I would have draped this gem over a silken cord and worn it around my neck 24 hours a day. I recommend one for your bedside table, one for your car, one for your desk, and one for everyone who cares about you."
— Andrea Gambill, Editor of *Bereavement* magazine

ISBN 978-1-879651-30-2 • 128 pages • softcover • $11.95

Companion
P R E S S

All Dr. Wolfelt's publications can be ordered by mail from:
Companion Press
3735 Broken Bow Road
Fort Collins, CO 80526
(970) 226-6050
www.centerforloss.com

ALSO BY ALAN WOLFELT

The Ten Essential Touchstones:

1. Open to the presence of your loss.
2. Dispel misconceptions about grief.
3. Embrace the uniqueness of your grief.
4. Explore your feelings of loss.
5. Recognize you are not crazy.
6. Understand the six needs of mourning.
7. Nurture yourself.
8. Reach out for help.
9. Seek reconciliation, not resolution.
10. Appreciate your transformation.

Understanding Your Grief
Ten Essential Touchstones for Finding Hope and Healing Your Heart

One of North America's leading grief educators, Dr. Alan Wolfelt has written many books about healing in grief. This book is his most comprehensive, covering the essential lessons that mourners have taught him in his three decades of working with the bereaved.

In compassionate, down-to-earth language, *Understanding Your Grief* describes ten touchstones—or trail markers—that are essential physical, emotional, cognitive, social, and spiritual signs for mourners to look for on their journey through grief.

Think of your grief as a wilderness—a vast, inhospitable forest. You must journey through this wilderness. To find your way out, you must become acquainted with its terrain and learn to follow the sometimes hard-to-find trail that leads to healing. In the wilderness of your grief, the touchstones are your trail markers. They are the signs that let you know you are on the right path. When you learn to identify and rely on the touchstones, you will find your way to hope and healing.

ISBN 978-1-879651-35-7 • 176 pages
softcover • $14.95

Companion
PRESS

All Dr. Wolfelt's publications can be ordered by mail from:
Companion Press
3735 Broken Bow Road
Fort Collins, CO 80526
(970) 226-6050
www.centerforloss.com

ALSO BY ALAN WOLFELT

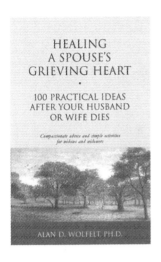

Healing a Spouse's Grieving Heart
100 Practical Ideas After Your Husband or Wife Dies

When your spouse dies, your loss is profound. Not only have you lost the companionship of someone you deeply loved, you have lost your helpmate, your lover, the person who shared your history, and perhaps your financial provider. Learning to cope with your grief and find continued meaning in life will be difficult, but you can and you will if you embrace the principles set down in this practical guide.

This book offers 100 practical, here-and-now suggestions for helping widows and widowers mourn well so they can go on to live well and love well again. Whether your spouse died recently or long ago, you will find comfort and healing in this compassionate book.

ISBN 978-1-879651-37-1 • 128 pages • softcover • $11.95

Companion
PRESS

All Dr. Wolfelt's publications can be ordered by mail from:
Companion Press
3735 Broken Bow Road
Fort Collins, CO 80526
(970) 226-6050
www.centerforloss.com

ALSO BY ALAN WOLFELT

Healing Your Grieving Heart After Stillbirth
100 Practical Ideas for Parents and Families

by Alan D. Wolfelt, Ph.D. and Raelynn Maloney, Ph.D.

The stillbirth of a hoped-for child is an inexplicable loss of hopes and dreams of a new life—to the parents, to the siblings this baby may have, to the extended family, and to friends. The impact of this overwhelming loss is profound and life-changing.

This compassionate guide contains 100 practical ideas to help those affected by the tragedy of stillbirth. Some of the ideas teach about the principles of grief and mourning. Others offer practical, action-oriented tips for coping with the natural difficulties of this loss, such as communication between spouses, explaining the death to others, reconciling anger or guilt, remembering the baby who died, and many others.

ISBN 978-1-61722-175-0 • 128 pages • softcover • $11.95

Companion
P R E S S

All Dr. Wolfelt's publications can be ordered by mail from:
Companion Press
3735 Broken Bow Road
Fort Collins, CO 80526
(970) 226-6050
www.centerforloss.com

ALSO BY ALAN WOLFELT

Finding the Words
How to Talk to Children and Teens About Death, Suicide, Funerals, Homicide, Cremation, and Other End-of-Life Matters

It's hard to talk to children and teens about death and dying, particularly when someone they love has died or might die soon. Our instinct as caring adults may be to shelter them from painful truths. Yet, as Dr. Wolfelt emphasizes, what kids need most is our honesty and our loving presence.

This practical and compassionate handbook includes dozens of suggested phrases to use with preschoolers, school-agers, and teenagers as you explain death in general or the death of a parent, a sibling, a grandparent, or a pet. Other chapters include possible words and ideas to draw on when you are talking to kids about a death by suicide, homicide, or terminal illness. At times, grown-ups must also have very difficult conversations with dying children; this book offers guidance. A final chapter discusses how to talk with kids about funerals, burial, and cremation.

ISBN 978-1-61722-189-7 • 144 pages • softcover • $14.95

Companion
PRESS

All Dr. Wolfelt's publications can be ordered by mail from:
Companion Press
3735 Broken Bow Road
Fort Collins, CO 80526
(970) 226-6050
www.centerforloss.com

TRAINING AND SPEAKING ENGAGEMENTS

To contact Dr. Wolfelt about speaking engagements or
training opportunities at his Center for Loss and Life Transition,
email him at DrWolfelt@centerforloss.com